# ZODIAC AND SWASTIKA

# ZODIAC AND SWASTIKA

HOW ASTROLOGY GUIDED HITLER'S GERMANY

WILHELM WULFF

*Foreword by Walter Laqueur*

Coward, McCann & Geoghegan, Inc.
NEW YORK

First American Edition 1973

First published in German under the title *Tierkreis und Hakenkreuz*

Copyright © 1968 by
Bertelsmann Sachbuchverlag Reinhard Mohn, Gütersloh

English translation copyright © 1973 by Arthur Barker, Ltd.

SBN: 698-10547-8

Library of Congress Catalog Card Number: 73-78733

PRINTED IN THE UNITED STATES OF AMERICA

# FOREWORD

by Walter Laqueur

"It is the stars above us who govern our conditions"—from the Chaldaeans to the Jungians, and most recently the American counterculture of the 1960's, astrology has had its practitioners, faithful believers and fellow travelers who thought it at least worthwhile to investigate the phenomenon noted by King Lear. Politicians and strategists in particular have been among the addicts, even though, as a rule, it did not do them much good. According to Josephus Flavius, the rebellion against Roman rule in Judaea came at the wrong time, as a result of astrological advice. Perhaps the most famous horoscope of all was Wallenstein's; he insisted on it, despite Kepler's warnings that it was quite pointless to look at the stars for causes and explanations of any kind of earthly event. How could he possibly know if Wallenstein would die from apoplexy, and whether this would happen abroad? If someone contracted venereal disease (Kepler wrote), was the planet Venus really responsible? But Wallenstein wanted his horoscope and Kepler needed money and so the transaction took place anyway. Beyond general statements Wallenstein wanted day-to-day guidance from the stars, and he installed Battista Senno, an Italian, as his private astrologer, who was to be available at any time of day or night. Senno participated in the conspiracy against Wallenstein which resulted in his murder. Nor have astrologists been of any apparent help to Mr. Sukarno or to certain Burmese rulers in our time.

Successful or not, astrology was practiced for many centuries; its heyday was in the Middle Ages when it was taught in many Italian universities. In the eighteenth century, however, it suffered a total eclipse and did not undergo a revival until around the turn of the century. As the European humanists had rediscovered the Greeks in the fifteenth century, so European astrologists uncovered Nostradamus, the Cabala (or what they thought represented it) and the Rosicrucian tradition. There was an astrologist revival in France and in England, but nowhere was the impact more strongly felt than in twentieth-century Germany.

There were more astrologists per square mile in Germany than in any other European country, to quote Ellic Howe's pioneering study *Urania's Children* (London, 1967). One of its adepts was Wilhelm Wulff, who, as a young art student before the first world war, had discovered astrological literature in Italy while doing research on Leonardo's drawings. He worked as a sculptor and astrologist in Hamburg, and through some of his clients, he came to know Kersten, who was Himmler's masseur and friend. Kersten, who appears in this book in a somewhat less savory light than in his own memoirs, put him in touch with high SS dignitaries, such as Nebe, Schellenberg and eventually Himmler. The Nazis took a dim view of astrology, which was suspect both for its Oriental origins and its universalist character; horoscopes that did not differentiate between Aryans and non-Aryans, between higher and inferior races could not possibly be accepted. Neither Hitler nor Goebbels, contrary to widespread belief, took astrology seriously, and its only official use was in German psychological warfare. A suitably edited version of Nostradamus' prophecies (which had originally appeared in 1568) was published, proving that Germany was to win the war. Unknown to the Germans, "Captain" Louis de Wohl was simultaneously preparing material in his Park Lane apartment for an Allied edition of Nostradamus which would prove exactly the opposite. Neither publication seems to have had a decisive influence on the course of the war.

Many German astrologers joined the Nazi party in 1933, but this did not help them; there was no room for rival ideologies in the Third Reich and Hitler had a monopoly, as far as political predictions were concerned. The astrological associations were dissolved, their journals gradually disappeared, and most astrologers were not permitted to practice. True, Nazi policy was not quite as consistent in this as it was in other respects; in certain regions of Germany the ban on astrology—as on jazz—was not strictly observed. As far as the Nazis were concerned, it was a marginal issue, and it was only after Hess' self-imposed mission to Scotland that the Gestapo stepped in and arrested all known active astrologers. Hess' circle included certain astrologers, and it was believed that they had somehow influenced the Führer's deputy. Among those arrested was Mr. Wulff, who spent four highly uncomfortable months in a concentration camp. Later he was forced to join one of the many "research institutes" which were part of the German war effort. One of his first major assignments was to locate Mussolini, who had disappeared following his ouster from power in 1943. Mr. Wulff claims to have provided the correct answer—about fifty miles southeast of Rome —at a time when no one else knew.

As the tide of the war turned against Germany, the SS leaders gradually became more interested in horoscopes, and their requests more and more embarrassing. Himmler wanted to know whether the Führer would live much longer and how he would die. By that time, at the latest, Mr. Wulff must have realized that he was skating on very thin ice indeed. Yet the worse the situation at the front line, the more he was in demand; during the last months of the war he had to be constantly in attendance. His account of his meetings with the leader of the SS does not offer any sensational new revelations, and it may be recommended as altogether reliable. It shows that lunacy in the higher ranks of the SS manifested itself in ·many ways, some of them quite unexpected.

Most of Mr. Wulff's readers will not be impressed by his theories. They will show no more sympathy to the "serious" astrologers (the category to which he belongs) than to the charlatans who have brought disrepute on the craft and whom he denounces. For neither the signs of the zodiac, nor the planets, nor the twelve houses seem to have provided much guidance to him in private life. Surely he must have looked at one time or another at his own horoscope; if so, it is difficult to understand how he could have overlooked the dangerous configuration and why, after 1933, he did not move as fast and as far away as possible from his own profession—and, above all, away from the SS leadership. It would have saved him a great deal of danger and unpleasantness. Inasmuch as the historical value of this account is concerned, such considerations are, of course, quite irrelevant. This book was not written to make converts, and in the last resort it does not matter in the least whether the horoscopes prepared by Mr. Wulff and his colleagues were correct, but rather whether the recipients believed in them and acted accordingly.

In Hamburg he had discovered a promising astrologer called Wulf, a student of poisons, Sanskrit, and other interesting subjects. Wulf's prophecies, as seen by Schellenberg in retrospect, seemed remarkably accurate. He had prophesied that Hitler would survive a great danger on 20th July 1944; that he would be ill in November 1944; and that he would die a mysterious death before 7th May 1945. His prophecies concerning Himmler were equally remarkable, though discreetly enveloped in diplomatic silence. Schellenberg found that in politics Wulf was sound; he introduced him to Himmler as a counterweight to the unsound Kaltenbrunner; and this introduction was so successful that before the end of the Third Reich, according to Schellenberg, "Himmler seldom took any steps without first consulting his horoscope."

—H. R. Trevor-Roper,
*The Last Days of Hitler*

# Contents

# Introduction: Why I Wrote This Book

One of the strangest features of the National Socialist regime was that while it persecuted astrologers and murdered some of them in concentration camps, it saw no harm in employing them for its own purposes at the same time. The fate of Karl Ernst Krafft, the Swiss astrologer, provides a tragic example. He was a strange and gifted man, a pioneer in the application of statistics to astrological investigations, and something of a mystic. He more or less emigrated from Zürich to the Black Forest district in southern Germany in 1937, largely because he felt that his abilities were not appreciated in Switzerland. He had an uncritical admiration for the Nazis and hoped to make a career of some kind in Germany. When the war began in September, 1939, he was on the point of returning to Switzerland but then changed his mind and remained in Germany. He was already acquainted with a junior member of Himmler's staff who worked in Section VII, which kept an eye on groups who were generally suspect as far as the Nazis were concerned: "fringe" religious sects, astrologers, occultists, former Freemasons, and so on. Section VII recruited him on a free-lance basis during the autumn of 1939 and then during the first week of 1940 brought him to Berlin, at the request of Dr.

Goebbels' Propaganda Ministry, to work on the prophecies of Michael Nostradamus, the famous sixteenth-
century French seer.

Krafft, however, soon regretted his connection with
Section VII and the Propaganda Ministry and during the
spring of 1940 found himself a job as a translator in the
Deutsche Nachrichtenbüro, the official government news
agency. Early in 1940 the British learned that Krafft was
in Berlin and immediately jumped to the completely
false conclusion that he *must* be working for Hitler.
Krafft never met Hitler—though he would have liked
nothing better—but he did achieve very brief contacts
with two important Nazi bosses, namely Dr. Hans Frank,
the governor-general of Poland, and Dr. Robert Ley, the
leader of the so-called Labor Front.

In June, 1941, a month after Rudolph Hess' dramatic
flight to Scotland, Krafft and hundreds of German astrologers were arrested. It was supposed that Hess had
received astrological advice prior to his departure. The
Gestapo was instructed to find the astrologer whom Hess
had allegedly consulted, but this mysterious person was
never identified, probably because he or she never ex-
isted. Almost all the arrested astrologers were released
after a few weeks or months, but Krafft was never freed;
he died at Buchenwald in January, 1945. I knew about
Krafft's imprisonment, but my efforts to help him were
in vain. Not even Himmler dared order his release without the Führer's approval.

Like nearly all my professional colleagues, I too was
severely persecuted from 1933 to 1945. Even before the
outbreak of war I had discovered what it meant to be
interrogated and imprisoned by the Gestapo, and after
Rudolf Hess' ill-starred flight to Scotland in 1941 I suf-

fered the same fate as the other German astrologers; I was arrested and taken to the infamous police prison in Hamburg—Fuhlsbüttel. It was thanks only to the machinations of an ambitious manufacturer and an old party member who worked for the SS and wanted to ingratiate himself with Himmler that I, just another concentration camp detainee, was employed by Himmler and his accomplices during the final phase of the war, and although this meant that I was released from prison, I was anything but a free man. On the contrary, I continued to live as a prisoner on an estate belonging to Himmler's masseur, Kersten, an estate which served as a secret work camp for specialists and, as such, was affiliated with the Ravensbrück concentration camp. I was no longer physically maltreated, but I worked under the constant threat of severe punishment should my calculations prove inaccurate.

All this happened at a time when the Nazi regime was facing certain defeat. Today it may well appear incongruous that the leaders of the "master race," who claimed to believe only in the race and its historical mission, should have suddenly placed their hopes in astrology, as if astrology were some secret weapon that could save them from their fate, and yet these events form part of this darkest chapter in German history.

The fact that I have now decided to set down my experiences in writing is not due to the promptings of friends or to the wishes of the publishers who have been urging me to do so for years. In fact, for any insight my readers may now gain into my life as an astrologer and into some of the events of recent German history, they will be indebted primarily to Hugh Trevor-Roper.

Trevor-Roper published his book *The Last Days of*

*Hitler* in London in 1947. It was soon translated into many languages and sold around the world. In this book both my name and the work that I did for Heinrich Himmler during the final phase of the war were mentioned on several occasions. The claims Trevor-Roper made about my activities included so much fantasy that I finally decided to speak. Let me give just one example. On page 93 of his book Trevor-Roper writes:

> In Hamburg he [Walter Schellenberg] had discovered a promising astrologer called Wulf, a student of poisons, Sanskrit, and other interesting subjects. Wulf's prophecies, as seen by Schellenberg in retrospect, seemed remarkably accurate. He had prophesied that Hitler would survive a great danger on 20th July 1944; that he would be ill in November 1944; and that he would die a mysterious death before 7th May 1945. His prophecies concerning Himmler were equally remarkable, though discreetly enveloped in diplomatic silence. Schellenberg found that in politics Wulf was sound; he introduced him to Himmler as a counterweight to the unsound Kaltenbrunner; and this introduction was so successful that before the end of the Third Reich, according to Schellenberg, "Himmler seldom took any steps without first consulting his horoscope."

Anyone reading this passage is forced to conclude not only that I was a sound Nazi but that I also fulfilled a function in the top circles surrounding Himmler which enabled me to oppose a man like Kaltenbrunner. It is time to set the record straight.

# CHAPTER 1

# I Become an Astrologer

In the spring of 1912 I was a young art student in Hamburg, uncertain of my future and perplexed by disagreements with my teachers. I greeted with delight my uncle's invitation to accompany him on his annual trip to southern Europe, without anticipating that this journey would change my life. We were to pass through the Alps to Lucerne, Geneva, Interlaken, Montreux, and then—to Italy.

Our trip proceeded uneventfully until, on the train near Basel, I ran into a friend of my uncle's, a priest named Monsignor von Berlichingen, who showed a keen interest in my artistic education and urged me to visit the Palazzo di Brera and the library in Milan, where, he explained, I could study the original drawings of Leonardo da Vinci. I took his advice, for I felt even then an enormous admiration for Leonardo. I was already aware that to study his work is to attend an academy not just of the fine arts but also of the mathematical and technical disciplines, in fact, of every aspect of the science of his time. I subsequently paid many visits to the Palazzo di Brera, yet though I saw the art academy, the picture gallery, and the entire library of unique ancient manuscripts, what struck me most of all was the astrology section. Of course there were other treasures there, but the collection of astrological books, far vaster than I had thought possible, was an untapped shrine which later scholars seemed to have passed over.

Although I had always had an interest in astrology, I had only, till then, had glimpses of answers to my many questions about it and about other peripheral spheres of human knowledge. Now, in the Palazzo di Brera, I was confronted by the astrological writings of the greatest medieval and ancient scientists.

Astrology has not always been held in ill repute. In ancient times it was not even regarded as an occult science; in fact, it provided the basis for the development of astronomy. Because of their joint origin it is difficult to distinguish between these two disciplines; from antiquity right up to the beginning of the modern era, we find important astronomers who are also astrologers: Ptolemy, Pierre d'Ailly, Johannes Kepler, and Morin de Villefranche. My research was not easy, for a study of astrology presupposes a working knowledge of more disciplines than one man can ever really master, among them classical languages, German and Oriental philology, history, art, religion, astronomy, and graphology.

During the course of my studies I found ancient books and manuscripts containing maps of the planets and constellations marked with the decanates—that is, the ten-degree subdivisions of the zodiac. I also found the traditional conception of the constellations well illustrated on both small panels and large paintings. My mind was filled with so many questions. Was it just superstition that had led man to regard the star-studded heaven as a human counselor for hundreds and even thousands of years? After all, man was able to calculate the seasons and the tides from the position of the stars with great accuracy, and there are cosmic events on which every living being depends for its existence. Is it not reasonable to assume, therefore, that if these elemental events are determined by the position of the stars, other incidents which also contribute to man's fate are determined in the same way? Roger Bacon, the great thirteenth-century Franciscan theologian and natural philosopher, censured medieval doctors for their ignorance of astrological matters: *"Et ideo negligunt meliorem partem medicinae"* ("And they neglect the better part of medicine"). Were such scholars deluded fools? This question gave me no peace, and so I decided to work far more intensively at my astrological studies.

I had an opportunity for further research when I spent several weeks in Munich on my way back from Italy. Among the things I wanted to see there was the horoscope which Kepler had cast for Wallenstein, the brilliant German general of the Thirty Years' War.

The Munich Hof- und Staatsbibliothek, as it then was, had several complete copies of Kepler's *Prognosticum*. This was just idle curiosity on my part, for at that time I understood precious little about horoscopes. I was all the more surprised, therefore, when a comparison with the historical events of Wallenstein's life showed Kepler's horoscope to be essentially correct. This discovery led me to begin calculating horoscopes for myself, and soon afterward I became a member of the Kepler Club in Hamburg, where I met a number of important people. I became friendly with one of the pioneers of the modern German astrological movement, Albert Kniepf. He shed greater light on the Wallenstein horoscope, for he had recalculated and corrected Kepler's work. Kniepf also drew my attention to a study by Dr. Ernst Brausewetter on Wallenstein and astrology. Wallenstein himself took an active interest in astrology, which may well have been prompted by practical considerations, for in the seventeenth century general astrological information was a substitute for military intelligence. It could take days or even weeks for a report to reach him, whereas regular astronomical observations at least enabled him to draw general conclusions for the day-to day conduct of affairs. In his study Brausewetter states that, as far as Wallenstein's personal fate was concerned, the wisdom of the astrologers, including Kepler, had been of no avail. This view is still widely held. It might therefore be profitable to deal with this question in greater detail.

Kepler cast Wallenstein's horoscope on two occasions, in 1608 and 1615, and was particularly successful in his general interpretation of the natal chart. Kepler concluded, among other things, that this nativity was very similar to the nativities of the late Chancellor of Poland and Queen Elizabeth of England, which also revealed many planets on the celestial horizon, rising on the ascendant or setting close to the descendant. "Consequently," he said, "there can be no doubt but that the man born at that time [Wallenstein] will achieve high dignities, riches, and a splendid marriage and that as a captain and revolutionary leader he will draw large numbers of soldiers to his person." It must be remembered that when Kepler cast this horoscope in 1608, he was dealing with an unknown nobleman who was barely twenty-five years of age. It was for such a man that he predicted a great career in the service of the state. He also spoke of the "many, great, harmful, public and secret enemies, over whom he will usually triumph." These are remarkable forecasts, which were complemented by sound conjectures as to the conditions and incidents of Wallenstein's future life.

The first natal chart that Kepler calculated for Wal-

lenstein cannot really be regarded as correct if we insist
on a precise knowledge of the "directions" (especially
the primary directions). Wallenstein had given Kepler a
wrong latitude reading for his place of birth, namely 51°
9′ N. This would have been approximately right for
Dresden, whereas Wallenstein was born on the estate of
Hermanitz near Arnau in Bohemia, which has a latitude
of 49° 56′ N. Despite the inaccuracy of his initial values
in 1608, Kepler nonetheless arrived at a generally correct
interpretation, which is a pretty rare feat and says much
for his ability in this sphere.

In 1624 Wallenstein had the first nativity corrected.
He wrote to Count Taxis: ". . . because some things were
set down too early, others too late . . . and because various mathematicians have agreed . . . that I am to live
outside the fatherland and also die there, and most of
them say that I am to die of apoplexy, I was curious to
hear what he [Kepler] had to say about it." In 1625
Kepler cast a new horoscope for Wallenstein based on
the corrected birth position. In it he listed the constellations which were ominous for Wallenstein and predicted
that "the cruel and terrible disorders in the state" would
be at their height in March, 1634. Wallenstein was murdered on February 25, 1634. Kepler was of course too
tactful to mention the general's death in his forecast for
1634. Instead, he spoke of terrible disorders. But it is
significant that the series of annual prognoses breaks off
with this observation!

Wallenstein paid the penalty for dismissing Kepler,
the best astrologer of his day, and replacing him with
mediocrities. In his *Astrologie* (1816), Professor J. W.
Pfaff, of the University of Erlangen, observed with some
justification that Wallenstein did not appreciate the true

significance of astrology but used it only to implement his political plans.

As a result of my encounter with Kepler's work in the year 1912, I was won over to astrology. For a long time I regarded this new departure as one of the sins of my youth. But it was one that I have never been able to renounce.

I came from a middle-class family of Hanseatic businessmen whose flair for honest commerce was shaped by the harbor, the docks, and the international trade of the city of Hamburg. Flood tides and launchings, naval visits and boat trips on the Alster and the Elbe formed the background to my childhood world. In that world I often heard of strange adventures of the kind met with in all coastal and harbor towns where sailors' and travelers' tales turn people's imaginations toward the unusual and even the supernatural. Fortune-tellers, clairvoyants, and mediums have always formed part of the substratum of Hamburg society. Such things have absolutely nothing to do with astrology, of course. And yet it may well be that I was predisposed from early childhood to accept the existence of special laws that could influence and even control our lives.

But this occult aspect of my environment was never really obtrusive. The dominant characteristic, both of the city at large and of my own family, was the rather cool and always extremely conventional tone of the Hanseatic business class. It was not surprising, therefore, that my father decided that I too was to become a businessman. He arranged for me to enter a well-known firm of Hamburg importers and exporters after I had passed my final school examination. He doubtless meant well and would certainly have found a suitable firm for my commercial training, which would have enabled me to take over his own firm when the time came. But my father had not reckoned with my deep-rooted aversion to commerce. Instead of taking up my post as an unpaid trainee, I fled to an isolated country village, which was then a painters' colony, to take counsel with my old teacher Paul Lichtwark, who had encouraged me to follow an artistic career. In the end my perseverance won the day, and after months of argument my father suddenly gave in. He allowed me to attend the new Hanseatic College for Fine Arts and agreed to pay for my studies.

When, in 1913, I showed some of my drawings, watercolors, sculptures, and masks to the director of the Hamburg School of Art, he suggested that I join one of the special classes at the school. And so I found myself studying under Johannes Bossard, from whom I learned some really useful sculpture techniques. But I soon began to feel that I was learning nothing at these classes and gave them up, immersing myself instead in my own work.

The outbreak of the First World War took me completely unawares. Luckily my call-up was deferred on medical grounds, and so for a time I was able to continue my studies. Most of my fellow students volunteered in that mood of national enthusiasm, were quickly trained, went to the front, and fell at Langemarck or Ypres or in Russia. Gradually the studios were emptied.

Finally, I too was conscripted. Neither the petitions of influential friends nor the intervention of my professor, Johannes Bossard, could save me from the drill of barracks life. But early in 1917 I was wounded and subsequently contracted typhus. I was discharged from the army and directed to work in an optics factory.

In my leisure hours I was able to take up my studies

again. This was made very much easier for me when I found a studio near the Alster, which provided me with the working atmosphere and the peace that I so desperately needed. Never had life seemed so cheerful, simple, and agreeable as in that sparsely furnished studio.

Nonetheless I longed for solitude, for seclusion far from modern civilization. Sometimes I even toyed with the idea of entering an order, hoping to find a monastic retreat for artists and scholars. Yet I continually asked myself whether a simple change of scene could cure my spiritual condition. My past seemed worthless, the future dreadful and terrifying in its uncertainty. In these, as in later crises, I was both strengthened and diverted by astrology. From the dominant constellations in my nativity I was able to understand why such crises were necessary and when they would pass. In fact, astrology taught me to understand life and to shape it to my ends.

But it was not until I met Heinrich Franck, a restaurant proprietor and former artist, that I became really deeply involved in astrology. His lean figure, his long, snow-white beard, and his shoulder-length, silver-gray hair struck me immediately when I saw him at an astrological gathering. At that time he was calculating ephemerides, or tables of planetary movements, and kindly offered to teach me this complex subject. He also owned an extensive library of old astrological and mystical books. With his help I learned to make valuable astronomical and astrological calculations and to cast horoscopes without reference to the English ephemerides, which were already known and used in Germany at that time. Each horoscope could be worked out mathematically without any help from tables of houses. Apart from his own library, Heinrich Franck also had a list of old astrological works owned by the Hamburg State Library and the Royal Library in Berlin, so that it was easy for me to obtain any books that I needed.

Meanwhile, the whole social climate threatened my precious artist's living. The war was ending, and inflation had begun to cast its first shadows over the economy. I could expect no real help from my father. I had chosen to be independent, and his firm was in financial trouble. Even some of the clients I managed to get refused to pay.

At this time my astrological studies were closely linked with my artistic work. When I was tired of modeling, painting, or drawing, my astrological studies helped revive my interest. But I had not yet realized that I could earn money with my astrological knowledge. And, of course, my abilities in this sphere were still very modest. For my first experiments in interpreting constellations I used my relatives and my intimate friends as guinea pigs. I was soon astonished to find that individual horoscopes corresponded remarkably to the character, talents, and circumstances of the persons concerned. I felt encouraged to calculate and analyze other horoscopes. I obtained details of the births of historical personalities whose lives had been well documented: Goethe, Kaiser Wilhelm I, Prince Otto von Bismarck, the Emperor Maximilian of Mexico, and Michelangelo. I learned a great deal from these studies. But one can become an ardent historian and astrologer from analyzing the horoscopes of famous men without ever feeling a personal involvement.

What really *is* exciting is to cast the horoscope of a living person one knows well and to make specific predictions, based on the evidence of his nativity, that are later proved true. It is, of course, positively frightening when one predicts illness or death. My younger brother's horoscope forecast a dangerous wound and the loss of a limb. I explained this to him early in 1913. No one thought it possible. In 1915 my brother was wounded by shrapnel in the trenches in France and had several operations. He lost his right leg.

During the long hours and days of waiting which are such a marked feature of army life and which most soldiers spend playing cards or drinking, I had plenty of time and opportunity to test my astrological knowledge. This was just a pastime, but all the same, it helped establish my astrological practice. Many of my comrades at the front and in the military hospital, whose horoscopes I had cast either for fun or out of curiosity, wrote to me after the war to ask for further predictions. At the same time a very special clientele began to appear, one that is to be found in astrological consulting rooms after every war and every catastrophe: unhappy mothers who had lost their sons on the battlefields, mothers of airmen who had been shot down, mothers who wanted to know whether sons who had been reported missing were still alive, and wives hoping to be told whether or when their husbands would return from prisoner-of-war camps. There were also women who simply came to tell me their troubles.

I was still fairly young, and although I knew from my own horoscope that these confidences placed in me by complete strangers were simply a predictable part of my career, I was always seized with compassion for such people.

Their personal sufferings were made even worse by the general political situation. The Germans had lost the war, imperial pomp was a thing of the past, a politically immature people had been engulfed by the November

Revolution of 1918, inflation was making headway, well-established businesses were crashing, and suicides were a daily event. In this period of tremendous economic and political uncertainty, hypnosis, mesmerism, clairvoyance, and every form of occultism flourished.* Such interests are promoted by catastrophic situations. In postwar Germany hypnotists, clairvoyants and mind readers were suddenly able to fill huge concert halls. There was scarcely a single large music hall or cabaret that did not stage a telepathic act. Enormous placards and newspaper advertisements pompously proclaimed: "The Most Important Parapsychologist," "The Woman with a Thousand Eyes" (Madame Karoli at the Busch Circus), "The Great Enigma, an Outstanding Achievement in the Sphere of Occult Science," "The Lady Who Tells You All," etc. Swindle or not, both public and press found it all fascinating. I was very soon revolted by this fairground occultism, and the more these things were discussed in public, the more I withdrew into the seclusion of my studio.

Meanwhile, the months passed quickly. During the spring and summer of 1919 revolutionary disturbances continued to flare up from time to time. Sometimes battles between workers and riot police took place right outside my studio. I paid little attention to such matters and saw no one. But my attempt to withdraw from the world failed. I was soon to come into contact with the political forces of the day. And I was destined to have further dealings with those very clairvoyants whose modish activities had seemed to me so repugnant.

One evening I received a totally unexpected visit from

---

* It seems, incidentally, that sections of American society were seized by a similar craze both during and after the American Civil War.

my father. This was the first time he had ever come to my studio; since I had decided to try my luck as a free-lance artist, he had not bothered about me very much. He was accompanied by two young men, former playmates of mine whom I had not seen for many years. They seemed very distressed and behaved as if under great pressure. They wanted to consult me on an astrological matter. It was ironical that they had been brought to me by my father, who had always maintained that there was nothing in my practice.

They then told me their story. Their sister had been missing for eight days. A few articles of clothing belonging to her had been found on a popular bathing beach on the upper Elbe; this had led them to fear the worst. My father hoped that with the help of astrological calculations I could at least give them some indication as to what had happened. But it would have taken days to obtain the necessary facts to draw up a horoscope, and the two men would not wait. As it happened, I had an appointment that evening with a doctor who wanted to carry out some experiments with a new medium whom he had discovered. And so I suggested that my visitors should accompany me there and that we use their sister's disappearance as a test case. Shortly afterward we made our way through the turbulent streets of the city to the doctor, who agreed to my proposal. I advised the brothers about the difficulties which could arise at such a séance and stressed the fact that the medium might conceivably possess no clairvoyant faculty at all. But this did not seem to bother them, and even my father decided to take part in the séance. He argued that my astrological calculations could be used to confirm or correct the clairvoyant's statements.

The brothers were eager to believe in the medium, and they were not, at first, disappointed. Soon after the doctor put him in a trance, the medium, who could not possibly have had any foreknowledge, gave an accurate description of the girl's appearance and habits and correctly revealed that she had been bathing with a man on a beach. The man was her fiancé. After hours of questioning the medium further revealed that the couple had stayed on the beach after the last boat, that the man had stabbed the girl to death, deposited her disfigured body on the bank, and, standing in the middle of the river, shot himself. We urged the medium to tell us the precise location of the corpses. He mumbled, "Lavenberg," a place which was highly improbable because of the tidal flow of the Elbe. The brothers were so desperate for any facts that they believed the medium and notified the police. The ensuing two-day search was fruitless. My father and I, on the other hand, had no faith at all in the medium.

Meanwhile, I had time to cast the horoscope of the missing girl. She had been born at Hamburg on July 26, 1892, at 7 P.M. Her natal chart showed the moon in a highly disadvantageous position and in conjunction with the malefic planet Saturn. Both were in the eighth house, the house of death, indicating both the manner and the place of death. Further, they were near Mercury, which in this horoscope was ruler of the fifth house, the house of emotion and love. Neptune, another malefic planet, was very badly placed in the fifth house. The coincidental deaths of the girl and her fiancé could be seen from the presence of Mercury, the moon, and Saturn in the eighth house. Saturn rules the ascendant in this horoscope. When Saturn is in the eighth house, it indicates that a person will be the cause of his or her own death. If, in this horoscope, we look at the subdivision of the zodiac as postulated in Indian astrology, we find the moon, Saturn, and Mars in watery Navāmšas (*i.e.*, a one-ninth or forty-degree sector of the zodiac) and Dvadašāmsas (one-twelfth or thirty-degree sector). And that means a watery grave—in this case suicide by drowning. I found no configuration which would have indicated the violent death suggested by the medium.

My interpretation proved to be essentially correct, even though it did not completely clear up the case. Three weeks later a fisherman found the corpses of the two missing persons a considerable distance downstream. The bodies revealed no injuries apart from a small scratch on the man's head which had been caused when the fisherman had pulled him ashore with a boathook. A farewell letter discovered shortly afterward furnished conclusive proof of a suicide pact. The engaged couple had been in great financial difficulties; the man had forged bills of exchange and embezzled considerable sums of money. After having exhausted their savings, they had decided to take their lives.

As a result of this and similar incidents, reports of my astrological prowess spread; people learned that I had begun to study Sanskrit so as to be able to use works of Indian astrology for my investigations. I myself have never tried to publicize my work either in advertisements or by giving lectures. Nonetheless, the number of people who visited me—not on account of my sculptures, but on account of my astrological interpretations—constantly grew, until a virtual professional practice developed in my studio.

In one of my early cases the central figure was a

woman who appeared to have been mysteriously murdered. The cheaper newspapers had seized on the affair
and blown it up into a sensational sex murder; this was,
of course, particularly disagreeable to the dead woman's
family. My astrological analysis indicated that it was not
a case of murder, but of accidental death, although the
detective inspector rejected my interpretation out of
hand. In his view the murderer was a well-known doctor,
who had tried to dispose of his victim's body in the most
atrocious way. The only evidence for this assumption
was the fact that the doctor had fled as soon as suspicion
had fallen on him. I rechecked my calculations but was
unable to draw any conclusion which would have enabled me to support the police theory. This case remained unsolved. Twenty-three years later it was shown
that the death really had been accidental. For reasons
which I never discovered, Reinhard Heydrich, the Gestapo chief, suddenly took up this old case, and by using
methods of crime detection such as only the Gestapo possessed, he succeeded in solving it. The lawyer defending
the alleged murderer let me have a look at the case files,
although he had no authority to do so. He was deeply
impressed that an astrological interpretation made more
than twenty years before had given the right lead for the
explanation of this unusual incident.

I did not take a fee for any of my investigations. Since
I looked upon myself as a professional sculptor, I would
have found it embarrassing and highly disagreeable to
have accepted payment for my special astrological skills.
And yet, because of those skills, my artistic work was
constantly interrupted, as was my dream of remaining a
recluse from the political forces of the age and the fash-
ionable whims of society.

CHAPTER 2

# Herbert Volck: The Embittered Veteran

A former officer, whom I had known at the front but had not seen for several years, appeared in my studio not long after the war was over. He had been an airman and later had joined the paramilitary Free Corps. He was the complete mercenary, a notorious troublemaker, and a nationalist who laid claim to the title of a "rebel for honor." His name was Herbert Volck. If I recount the circumstances of his life in some detail, it is not just because he sought my friendship for years on end or because I constantly found myself involved in some way in his activities. I do so because Volck is a good example of the generation of German soldiers who had been unable to accept the capitulation and regarded the Weimar Republic as a national disgrace. Through him I gained an intimate knowledge of the right-wing radicals who opposed not only the Communists but all forms of political sanity. Following the politically inept Treaty of Versailles, which had such unfortunate repercussions both for Germany and for the rest of the world, these people continued the war inside the republic, employing terrorist measures which paved the way for the National Socialists.

I do not remember exactly when I first met Herbert

Volck. It must have been about 1915, either in the Rokitno marshes in the Ukraine, where Volck was later shot down, or else in Danzig on a horse convoy. Volck was always cheerful, healthy, and athletic, a practical joker who paid little attention to army regulations. He wanted no more than to be a soldier and could not be bothered with "intellectual nonsense."

About four years later he suddenly appeared in my studio. Somewhere in Russia I had once told him a little about his future and about the dangerous years which lay ahead of him. Although he had then scoffed at my pessimism, he was now intrigued by my forecasts. Above all, of course, he wanted to know about his future. He asked me whether he should discard his uniform, turn civilian, and push a pen in an office. For Herbert Volck the war had not come to an end on November 11, 1918. He had been in Berlin when the armistice was declared but shortly afterward went to Lüneburg Heath at his father's request to muster a unit to fight against the Bolsheviks in the Baltic provinces. This Free Corps unit, which called itself the "Iron Brigade," went with Volck to fight in his Baltic homeland. I have no wish to condemn the Free Corps as such, but Volck's brigade was utterly useless as a military force, and this whole undertaking was just one of the many senseless ventures which he perpetrated in the course of his life. Shortly before his troop was due to be disbanded, he returned to Germany wounded in the arm. Later it was rumored that he had taken the regimental funds with him for safekeeping.

Volck had never had any money, and yet, as he stood before me with his arm in a sling, he seemed to have access to enormous sums and could afford to convalesce in an expensive sanatorium on the Baltic coast. Standing before me in a spotless new Iron Brigade uniform, his chest covered with medals, he asked me to tell him his future. I had already sketched out the salient points for him, suggesting that he take up a civilian occupation or become a writer. He would certainly have been able to write an interesting book on his wartime and postwar experiences. But Volck wanted to remain an officer and even hinted at offering his services to a foreign army. He suddenly conceived two startling ideas: one was to give lectures on the Caucasus, in America; the other was to open a detective agency in Germany. I thought these projects were mere fantasies, but, surprisingly, he went ahead with both. I heard him declaiming the sort of phrases that were to infect our whole nation within a few years. He liked to talk about his wartime experiences and did so at great length, but he said very little about his Baltic volunteer corps, "which fate snatched from my hands," presumably because he had stolen the regimental funds.

Before setting out for the United States, Volck did publish a book. But he spurned my advice to give up his military and political activities and work off his fantasies by writing detective novels. And he continued to live dangerously. One day he brought me the birth data of a man who, he said, had one foot in London and the other in the Soviet embassy in Berlin. This man pretended that his name was Pinkelée, but it emerged that this was a cover name for Sir Basil Zaharoff, the Levantine arms king and probably the greatest arms dealer of all time. Zaharoff was buying up former German war matériel with inflation currency. His requirements were insatiable, because he supplied the stuff for every civil war, revolution, and partisan struggle that flared up in the world after 1918. Volck knew about the secret weapon dumps set up by the paramilitary and Free Corps groups and was trying to get in on these arms deals, which were worth millions.

But his intrigues had always been regarded as suspect by the republican government in Berlin, and various government departments made life as difficult as possible for him and his detective agency. Perhaps this was one reason why he hated democracy and despised the "Weimar system."

Volck decided, in the early summer of 1922, to set out on his long-planned journey to America. Strangely enough, although my astrological forecasts for this venture were decidedly gloomy, I found myself wishing Herbert Volck good luck on his journey. Initially he had good luck, for his ship was just seven days out to sea when Walther Rathenau was murdered in Berlin, five months after he had become German Foreign Minister. Volck had been in contact with the assassins, but his financial difficulties had prevented him from becoming involved in this affair.

A fortune-teller had predicted great success for Volck in America, but it was my own negative astrological forecast that proved correct. His journey to the United States ended in fiasco. He was officially traveling on detective-agency business, trying to track down a stolen Rembrandt. He was, in fact, supporting himself by lecturing to the many German clubs in America on his wartime experiences. But he did not stop there. He told fantastic, inflammatory stories about the intrigues of the "cosmopolitan powers," a supposed conspiracy of Jewish financiers. He even claimed to have discovered a "hot-line" telephone connection between the White House and the banker J. P. Morgan. This almost caused a scandal, and both the German and American governments decided to put a stop to his demagoguery. Volck was forced to return to Germany.

But his journey had not been a complete waste of time, for he had used a tip from the Hamburg underworld to identify the Rembrandt thief. This was quite a success for a dilettante private detective and brought him some fame which would have been useful for his future practice. But he squandered his good fortune by continuing to make political speeches and getting himself and his partner heavily in debt. About a year after his return from America, in the summer of 1923, I met Volck and his wife on the Leipzig–Hamburg express. I was returning from a second postwar astrologers' conference, and I was preoccupied with excitement at the thought of potential developments in German astrology. But I was sharply struck by Volck when I realized he had become almost a megalomaniac. In a visit shortly after that meeting he began to enthuse over a new political movement—the National Socialists.

Today I have to ask myself why I did not simply throw this tedious braggart and agitator out on his ear. The reason is really quite simple. For me Volck was an interesting astrological case, and the more I saw of him and his world, the more fascinated I became. Volck even appealed to me as a sculptor. He was a good head and sometimes sat for me as a model.

On one such occasion, while I worked silently at his bust, he spent hours explaining the aims and ideals of the National Socialist movement to me and the young woman who later became his second wife. He had also brought the birth data of Hitler, Göring, and Röhm with him from Munich and asked me whether the putsch they were planning was likely to succeed.

At Volck's request I first cast Hitler's horoscope in August, 1923. In it I found particularly unfavorable planetary combinations, and for the autumn of 1923 Hitler's ascendant revealed a malefic conjunction of Saturn and Mars. For about twenty-four hours on or about November 8–9, Mars and Saturn were particularly threatening. There were indications of violence with a disastrous outcome. The horoscopes of Hitler and Herbert Volck were catastrophically opposed to each other. Consequently I advised Volck to have no further dealings with these new political friends. But, as usual, he spurned my advice.

I pointed this out to Volck: "If Saturn occupies the worst position (Leo) in the tenth house without being in aspect with benevolent planets, the person concerned will become a leader of 'coolies.' He will issue senseless and cruel orders and will be feared." I handed this text to Volck together with other observations on Hitler's horoscope and asked him if he really wanted to become one of Hitler's coolies. I reminded him that the coolie, in ancient Sanskrit texts a Sudra, is a member of the lowest Indian caste. Volck said nothing, but seemed impressed. We never mentioned the subject again, and I thought that I had convinced him. I was mistaken. Although Volck did not spend the next few years in the ranks of the Nazi Party, he wrote loyal addresses and begging letters to Röhm, Göring, and Adolf Hitler as soon as the Nazis came to power in 1933.

My interpretation of Hitler's horoscope was later discovered and seized by the Gestapo when they were searching my house, and I was arrested. These low-ranking Gestapo officials were particularly incensed by this find. Years later, about 1941, Heydrich asked me whether I would be prepared to supply a more detailed interpretation of this horoscope. Himmler, who was present at the time, said nothing but gave a broad grin. He had already read my interpretation with great enjoyment.

In October, 1923, Volck visited central Germany and Stuttgart and returned with ominous news of a revolutionary conspiracy, and in this particular instance Volck's statements, although they sounded fantastic, were not without foundation. Between the middle of October and November 9, 1923, revolts flared up all over Germany— first in Saxony and Thuringia, where troops were used against the socialist governments, and finally in Munich, where Hitler's and Ludendorff's march on the Feldherrnhalle was designed to topple the Bavarian, if not indeed the German, government. Hamburg was not spared either. A Communist uprising raged in the city from October 22–24, 1923, before the police brutally suppressed it. Volck's mind was uneasy. During the Hamburg revolt he slipped into my flat to ask me if the Weimar government would be able to hold out just a little longer. Suddenly he found the hated republican government more agreeable than a victory for the people who he had learned had him on their extermination list. The astrological consultation was brief. I told him he would get nothing out of a republican government. He then left me and disappeared into the tumult of the street battles.

Later that same evening he reappeared, accompanied by a plump, squat man in country clothes, with sharp, observant eyes. This man said scarcely a word. He stood inspecting my room while Volck explained the situation to me. The fighting had reached a climax in the city, and he had been unable to reach his flat in the Sierichstrasse. He would be grateful, therefore, if I would give shelter to him and his companion for the night. After I had agreed, Volck introduced the man. It was Martin Bormann, whom Volck had met on an estate in Mecklenburg. That night Volck was very nervous; he telephoned the police command posts several times, but all he could discover was that the battle was still undecided. I made an astrological calculation and was able to put his mind at rest. According to my forecast, the police would have everything under control by the next day, without having to call in the Hamburg citizens' militia. And so it was. At noon, when Herbert Volck and Martin Bormann left my flat, the street battles were virtually over. Martin Bormann had scarcely spoken three words to me. He had sat shyly at the end of the sofa with a forbidding expression on his face, a man who put up an impenetrable front and played his cards very close to his chest. I never saw Martin Bormann again.

After this turbulent summer and autumn things quieted down fairly quickly, primarily because the currency was stabilized at the end of 1923. Immediately afterward, heavy foreign investment led to an economic recovery which, although it proved unreal in the end, nonetheless afforded a good breathing space. Volck now turned his attention to building up his detective agency. It would take too long to enumerate all the cases, both big and small, for which Volck enlisted my astrological services in those days and for which, incidentally, he never once offered me a fee. I still have the astrological calculations which I made for Volck at that time. They run to several volumes. But I should like to recount just one case in which I used a particular astrological technique that proved successful on a subsequent and much more important occasion and may even have saved my life. The case involved a large haul of jewels which had been stolen from the Hamburg villa of a world-famous dealer in precious stones. I consulted my stellar chronometer, and from the constellation which it revealed, I could tell that the whole of the haul was still in the jeweler's house and that neither the members of his family nor outside agents had been involved in the affair.

The constellation indicated that the maid had carried out the robbery and hidden or perhaps buried the jewels near a water tank in the cellar of the house. Volck took this information to the police, the maid was interrogated, and the stolen jewels were discovered in the cellar. The maid was the mistress of a local gang leader whom the police had been trying to catch for some time. As a result of this case, the police were able to clear up a second robbery involving a sum of 300,000 marks which had been stolen from the strong room of the racetrack in Hamburg-Farmsen.

The fact that my forecast had not only proved correct but was the sole evidence available to the police in the solution of this particular crime may seem incredible to the reader. At best he is likely to regard the whole affair as a lucky coincidence which happened to corroborate my prediction. But my knowledge was not based on chance or on any mysterious circumstances. Readers who know any astrology will realize that it *is* possible to make specific statements of this kind from the interpretation of astrological data. The method involved can be learned by anyone prepared to make the necessary effort. I have often carried out experiments of this kind, and they have nearly always been successful. The most spectacular case

was that concerning Mussolini's capture in the summer
of 1943 and the subsequent search for his place of imprisonment. I will deal with the search for Mussolini in a
later chapter.

In November, 1928, a man called at my home. He was
a giant, with enormous hands evidently accustomed to
hard work. Without introducing himself, he began immediately to ask me a number of questions about my
"trade." He visited me again shortly, accompanied by
Volck, whom he described as his wartime comrade and
adjutant. This time I found out that his name was Claus
Heim. Heim told me that he was a member of the ex-
treme right-wing Schleswig-Holstein farmers' movement,
which had been formed to combat the very heavy taxes
and mortgages imposed on the almost bankrupt farmers
in that region. Volck had been hired as a soapbox orator
to drum up support for the resistance among these farmers, and he and Heim were planning their attack on the
local bailiffs and rural administration centers.

Volck and Heim were probably thinking of using ex-
plosives, although they said nothing about it to me. But a
horary horoscope showed me what they intended, and I
warned them against the use of violence, telling them
that their constellations were particularly unfavorable
for any such undertakings. I said that they could both
expect to be tried as criminals and that Heim might well
receive a long prison sentence. But both Claus Heim and
Herbert Volck believed nonviolent action to be useless.
At that point I asked them to leave my house since I
wanted nothing to do with violent protest.

A little later I cast a very detailed general horoscope
for Volck in which I told him that his luck would have
run out by July, 1929, and that he would probably find

himself behind bars. I told him that in July, 1929, the constellation which had been present at the time when he was taken prisoner in Russia would reemerge and would remain operative until October. Meanwhile, during the winter of 1928–29 and the following spring and summer, a large number of protest demonstrations and bomb attacks on the tax and rural administration offices took place in quick succession. By the autumn of 1929 the police had launched a vigorous drive to catch the terrorists, and a tip-off about a car used in the attacks led them to Heim and Volck. Volck managed to get out of the country on the pretext of a honeymoon with his second wife, but he was enticed back to Germany by a business offer, and soon both men were behind bars.

As a result of Volck's arrest and the proceedings taken against him and the other terrorists, the press began to show an interest in me, which I found extremely disagreeable. Prior to Volck's arrest I had actually been taken into custody for a short while because the police had found in his mother's house letters of mine addressed to Volck, together with a number of horoscope interpretations. Since they had also found my Hamburg address, I was arrested immediately (on September 29, 1929). The police confiscated my diary for the year 1929 because it contained horoscope calculations for Volck; they also discovered the addresses and telephone numbers of various members of the farmers' movement. My protest, in which I claimed the same right to secrecy in respect of confidential information accorded to every doctor, minister of religion, and lawyer, was completely ignored, and I was not even allowed to telephone my lawyer. Soon the tabloid press of Berlin went to work. *Vossischen Zeitung* stated: "There can be no doubt that Volck acted under

Wulff's influence." Later, when Volck and Heim were standing trial, the press launched further attacks. For example, the *Echo* wrote: "It was established that in the bomb outrage of November 27, 1928 in the Winsen tax office the idea for the plot stemmed from Herbert Volck, who had been led to perpetrate such acts of violence as a result of his preoccupation with astrology and other mystical matters."

Headlines such as THE TERRORISTS CONSULT THE ASTROLOGER, THE HOROSCOPE OF BOMB OUTRAGES, and THE TERRORISTS CONSULT THE FORTUNE-TELLER filled the newspapers. The *Kieler Volkszeitung* and the *Hannoverschen Zeitung* printed similar sentiments: "It seems clear that the various bomb outrages were based on horoscopes and astrological data." I often wished that I had never set eyes on Volck.

On October 31, 1930, Volck and Heim were sentenced to seven years' hard labor. But Volck was not destined to remain in prison long. A chronic case of scurvy he had developed in the first war worsened through the lack of medical treatment in prison, and the authorities then tried to bury his politically awkward case by depositing him in a state mental hospital in Göttingen. Only the fast work of Volck's lawyer saved him, and at Christmas, 1930, he was released on medical grounds. However, Volck had not learned his lesson. He retired for almost a year to a Baltic spa, but a letter I received from him in October, 1931, revealed his restlessness: "What do you think of that filthy Reichstag business? It's time the voice of the nation was heard. As soon as the bomb affair dies down, friends of mine intend to get me an important political post."

He was once again entering a dangerous political arena

in which he could have been arrested at a moment's notice. He refused the offer of a new refuge from a friend of
mine when he learned he would not be allowed to use the
retreat as a base for propaganda. Then, on January 16,
1932, he was ordered to the Gollnow prison to complete
his sentence.

Volck besieged me with appeals for help and requests
for new astrological calculations to discover how long any
further term of imprisonment might last. I had already
prepared a detailed astrological report at the time of the
trial, which had given no indication of long imprisonment, but Volck always forgot my forecasts very quickly.
I made a new calculation which made it clear that he
would be released on or about July 22, 1932. Once again
my astrological predictions were borne out. On August 1,
1932, Volck was informed by special messenger that he
had been given a conditional discharge on medical
grounds.

He was no sooner free than he rushed back into politics
with characteristic impetuosity. He could scent a "new
dawn." The "brown horde" was on the move, "the national rebellion was under way," and he could not afford
to miss it. For his "conquest of Berlin," he rented a very
attractive flat in Potsdam, where he invited me to visit
him in May, 1933. He suggested that I join him in Berlin.
He was sure that I would be able to build up a flourish-
ing astrological practice there. But as far as I could see,
what he really wanted was a personal adviser constantly
on hand.

This offer was not acceptable to me, for I knew Volck
too well to put any faith in his disinterestedness. In a
letter to me Volck claimed that he had given Göring the
idea for the Gestapo. Now he was complaining that this

had not led to a high appointment and that Heydrich had been put in charge of the Gestapo. He also wrote, "It is rumored that the first phase of Nazi rule is reaching its peak and that the many unsuitable people who exploited it will soon be replaced. I have the feeling that men of my kind will have to be brought in." Volck had always been optimistic about his political career. His lust for power, his ambition, and his almost unbelievable vanity and presumption, coupled with his low intelligence, invariably led him to assess political situations in terms highly favorable to himself. But in this case he was correct. The "exploiters" not only were replaced, but were completely eradicated. On June 30, 1934, when Röhm and a large number of the SA leaders were murdered by Hitler, their fate was shared by many other political activists who had incurred official displeasure. Volck was carried along by the "national revolution." Soon he was performing secret missions for the Gestapo, the SA, and the SS.

Meanwhile, the worsening economic situation had created further problems for me. My family's import-export business had been hard hit by the foreign currency regulations, and besides, I was officially forbidden to work as an astrologer. At first this veto applied only to Greater Berlin, but since many of my friends and clients thought I was no longer casting horoscopes, I was virtually unemployed. For a while astrologers who could produce the diploma of the Astrological Center at Düsseldorf were able to continue their work without hindrance in the administrative districts of Cologne, Düsseldorf, and Hamburg. But the insidious propaganda campaign launched by the Nazis persuaded people that it was better to give up consulting astrologers than run the risk of interrogation by the Gestapo. Consequently I was forced

to dispose of my valuables, including a number of paintings and pieces of antique furniture which I had inherited. Herbert Volck was too preoccupied with himself
and his own career to spare a thought for my material
difficulties, let alone stand by me, although, according to
well-informed sources, he was now receiving a princely
income.

Volck's greatest ambition was to make personal contact
with Hitler, whom he had been unable to reach so far
because his path had been blocked by "party members
who always feared that others, whose achievements were
greater than their own, would make an impression on
Hitler." I had told him time and again that any connection with Hitler would be an unmitigated disaster for
him since, in Hitler's horoscope, the malefic planet Saturn was in Leo, while in Volck's chart Leo was on the
ascendant. There were also several other constellations in
their respective horoscopes whose interactions would
prove harmful. Consequently personal contact between
Volck and Hitler was to be discouraged at all costs. Hitler
had in any case declared that he could not abide this
"Baltic seigneur" (Volck). But despite this assessment,
Volck insisted on running after him.

Needless to say, his attempts to reach Hitler ended in
failure, just as had his earlier attempts to curry favor with
Röhm. Although Volck knew as early as 1923 that I had
no sympathy for Hitler and his followers, he asked me
time and again whether, in astrological terms, there was
not, after all, some hope that he might establish contact
with his idols.

The dreadful predictions which I had made in respect
to the Hitler regime became reality only too soon. Hitler's Saturn spanned my own horoscope too, and at that
time my own constellations were extremely disadvan-

tageous. Saturn was transiting my tenth house (profession, occupation, etc.) and in the worst possible aspect to my radical Mars and other planets in my natal horoscope. Uranus, the planet associated with revolutions, was transiting my Jupiter. Jupiter symbolizes the happiness and well-being of humanity. Neptune was in bad aspect to my ascendant. My calculations showed that the summer of 1934 would be a bad period. I was not mistaken. There was the terrible series of murders perpetrated on June 30, 1934, in connection with the so-called Röhm Putsch. The authorities insisted that murder was necessary for the defense of the realm, but what they achieved was the destruction of the whole basis of constitutional order and personal liberty. Justice became a synonym for naked force.

I was deeply shaken, even though I had predicted from my astrological calculations that something of the sort was bound to happen, and I had also learned, from Volck, about the tensions between Hitler and Röhm. Heydrich's great moment had now come; he was appointed head of the Secret Police. Since Volck was working in close collaboration with Heydrich in 1934, he hoped that he would at least obtain the post of head of the Berlin Police—he would have liked best of all to have been in Heydrich's place himself, but he hoped in vain.

In Volck's horoscope Saturn, the planet of misfortune, was transiting the seventh house. This meant that Volck was likely to form dangerous connections with depraved and unreliable people. I reminded Volck of this and warned him to avoid all indiscreet contacts. By this time, of course, Volck knew enough about astrology to have realized for himself the implications of this Saturn transit for the years 1933–34.

We were having coffee on the terrace one afternoon,

when Volck began to lecture me again on the political situation. He spoke of the dangers which had arisen following June 30, 1934, and inveighed against Hindenburg, who was already a sick man. He had retired to his estate, which had been cordoned off by SS detachments for his "protection." Volck thought Hindenburg was too senile to start a political fight; very soon the Nazis would take the initiative, and everything that was impure and racially worthless would disappear. Volck then expounded the new philosophy which he had apparently absorbed in a training course.

He used phrases like: "We are investigating the soul of the nation!" and "With us there is no violation of the law for the sake of political expediency!" His affected Nazi manner revolted me. I was about to interrupt his emotional and undigested twaddle, of which I had had more than my share in the past, when he suddenly said to me, "You must now work for us!"

I was startled and asked, "What do you mean 'for us'? For Hitler and his murderers?" I reminded him of my astrological forecasts for Hitler and his followers.

To this he retorted angrily, "We have our own methods of making people work for us. If you should refuse, I can force you to do so. The only thing that can save you is total submission to the National Socialist doctrine. Do you understand?" I said nothing and remained calm. He continued, "Those who refuse to accept National Socialism and its ideology will die! Hitler demands that we should submit to his law!" I gave Volck a long hard look. But he went on to threaten me—his friend—in unmistakable terms: "If you don't join us, the curse of the National Socialist community will strike you down." By now Volck's face had contorted into a grimace. "We can soon have your head lopped off," he said. Secret executions were of course just a "military exercise" for Volck and his ilk.

At that moment my only thought was that Volck's obsession would drive him mad. There had been many occasions in my life when my hot temper had got the better of me. But at that moment, when Volck was prepared to deal a despicable blow to an old friend, I retained complete control of myself even though I was consumed with rage.

That evening, when Volck had started off again about his mysterious activities, I had a talk with his wife, a hysterical woman who told me that she was a medium and a clairvoyant. Her background was middle class, and because of her own pathological ambition, she encouraged Volck in his grandiose plans instead of trying to dissuade him. Edda Volck was pregnant and wanted a "child of pure descent, a noble scion." She was also anxious to know from me whether everything would work out well for her.

I could tell her nothing comforting, because her stars were very ominous. She eventually miscarried.

Some time later, although I was still annoyed with Volck, I accepted an invitation to dine at his house together with my friend Dr. Henry Goverts, the publisher, who had driven me to Berlin. The following evening I collected Dr. Goverts from his hotel and took him to Volck's house. A friend of ours, Carlo Mierendorf, had been sent to a concentration camp, and Goverts was hoping to persuade Volck to arrange for his release. After the customary examination of the tasteless and ostentatious flat, which, naturally, called for appropriate murmurs of approval for the highly polished Louis Seize style bed-

room suite, the "ancestral portraits" in the drawing room
and the "old German" dining room, we were invited to
dine. Toward the end of the meal we heard a squeal of
brakes as a car pulled up outside the house. Volck listened, looked out of the window, and turned pale. Then
I saw him going for the pistol which he always carried in
his jacket. I heard him release the safety catch. Before we
knew what had happened, two men—they were Gestapo
officials—stood at the door with pistols trained on Volck.
I was afraid that Volck would shoot, and so I knocked the
gun from his hand. He was trembling from head to foot.
The smaller of the two Gestapo officials, a thickset man
with cold, beady eyes, approached Volck from behind
and in a great booming voice ordered him to produce his
papers. Everything happened very quickly. Without
wasting another word, they led Volck off in handcuffs,
while two other secret policemen "took care" of his wife.
Goverts and I were also taken and traveled in the Gestapo truck through the nocturnal streets to the "Alex,"
the main Gestapo building in Berlin, where we were
placed in separate rooms on the third floor. There we
waited. Eventually I was brought before Heydrich for
interrogation. All that I learned from the interrogation
was that Volck had again become involved in some shady
business. It was only years later that I was told what had
actually happened. He had been associated with an elegant young lady, Gräfin von der Schulenburg, who had
engaged in espionage with the Russians. Volck had been
arrested on the same charge. Just how deeply he was involved I never discovered. I do not know whether he was
a victim of his own stupidity or of one of Heydrich's dev-
ilish tricks.

It was well known that Heydrich was collecting incrim-

inating evidence against many people in the Third
Reich. Volck had been sufficiently indiscreet to talk
about his hopes of becoming head of the Berlin Police
Force and perhaps even head of the Secret Police. Since,
at that time, Heydrich had the same idea, Volck was in
his way. Once Volck had been eliminated as a possible
rival, he made an ideal puppet for Heydrich. Heydrich
had collected enough evidence against this "rebel" to
make him compliant. Volck was a "Nordic" type and
Heydrich had a "Nordic" complex. He wanted only pure
"Germanic" types in his entourage, from whom he demanded unswerving loyalty and absolute obedience. His
men had to function without hestiation and without
scruple.

But, of course, Volck's hopes of establishing personal
contact with Hitler had now been completely frustrated.
This vain, ambitious, reckless, and unintelligent man was
no match for the sober, cold-blooded, and calculating
Heydrich. The only qualities which these two had in
common were their boundless ambition and their lust for
power.

Dr. Goverts, who was also interrogated by Heydrich,
naturally knew even less than I, and so Heydrich soon
arranged for us to be driven home in a private car. As we
walked down the long corridor of the Gestapo headquarters toward the exit, we caught sight of Volck in the distance being conducted in chains to the basement, where
the cells were situated. That was the last we ever saw of
him.

In fact, Volck was released shortly afterward and went
on a holiday to Switzerland. In 1935 and 1936 he worked
"for Germany" in the Eger district of Czechoslovakia,
then toured Austria as a speaker for the German organi-

zation responsible for "the education of the people," visiting Vienna, Graz, Salzburg, and Linz in the process. In May, 1939, I was told that Volck was "marching on the victory trail." When war was declared on Poland, he reported to the Luftwaffe at Kolberg in Pomerania. Later he is said to have been active in Budapest. He probably never realized that his cold-blooded and powerful rival Heydrich had already settled his score in 1934 and that from then on he had simply been a tool in the hands of this demon in SS uniform. Heydrich was assassinated by Czech resistance fighters in Prague in 1942. Volck did not survive him for very long. Although the circumstances surrounding his death are obscure, it seems that he must have fallen into disfavor with the Nazi powers; Herbert Volck was executed in Buchenwald concentration camp in August, 1944.

# CHAPTER 3

# Captain Lohmann: Rearmament by Stealth

A man like Volck was a lone wolf; he acted on his own and planned his reckless escapades for personal or financial advantage, hoping to ensure their success with the help of astrology. But another man who consulted me was just as deeply involved in the approaching disaster, though in a way that appeared more legitimate and certainly more intelligent.

Walter Lohmann, a former naval captain, worked for the Intelligence Service in the Weimar Republic. He was chiefly concerned with Eastern espionage and was a section head in the Navy Department, which at that time came under the jurisdiction of the War Ministry. It must have been in the winter of 1925–26 that Lohmann first contacted me. He remained my client until his death in 1930.

Both the timing and the manner of this contact were entirely typical. First Lohmann sent an associate with examples of his handwriting. A few weeks later I met him in person. In the immediate postwar period Lohmann's work had involved the implementation of the armistice conditions. When I met him, this work appeared to be at an end. As an officer in a defeated army which had been reduced to 100,000 men, Lohmann was far from sanguine about his future, although it seemed to me that he had not fully appreciated the potential of his new post in the Intelligence Service. He had realized that to be successful, a modern counterespionage service had to protect the masses from ideological infiltration. For this reason he wanted to make new-style propaganda films. He had first conceived the idea under the impact of the great Soviet films of the 1920's. Einstein's *Battleship Potemkin* was not only an artistic milestone in the history of the cinema, but also a great piece of Communist propaganda. The combination of the new close-up technique with crowd scenes produced contrast effects which were both exciting and highly suggestive; the bourgeois public of the Western world was deeply moved by the revolutionary pathos of this film. At its German premiere, in one of the large cinemas in Berlin, the audience stood up at the end of the performance and shouted, "Long live Moscow! Long live world revolution!"

It was this experience that had prompted Lohmann to consider the possibility of using the German film industry for "patriotic" purposes. He wanted to produce artistic films which would propagate the image of a "good Germany" both at home and abroad. To us, today, it seems almost as if Captain Lohmann were anticipating the *Kulturpolitik* of Dr. Goebbels, who harnessed the whole of the German film industry for purposes of nationalist propaganda within a few years of Lohmann's death. However, Lohmann's aims were far less ambitious. He was no National Socialist "minister of culture." He merely wished to serve the interests of his country by developing new lines of access to the public. Today this development may strike us as mistaken and dangerous. But the Lohmann affair shows the sort of ideas that were in the air in Germany barely ten years before the National Socialists came to power. It also illustrates the process by which the German Officer Corps, which was supposed to be entirely neutral, was becoming more and more political, partly because of dissatisfaction with its own status, partly as a result of the pressures brought to bear on it by the instability of the state.

And so Lohmann decided to make films. But of course this sort of project could not be undertaken either by the Reichswehr (the army) or by the government. Consequently the German film industry had to be won over, and this demanded guaranteed financial backing which could only be arranged if the government were prepared to underwrite the necessary bank loans.

Lohmann decided that the best way to realize his project and retain control of it was to acquire a majority interest in a film company, the sort of interest normally held by a backer. The Phoebus Film Company, a competent but undercapitalized concern whose offices were situated next to the Naval Department on the Bendlerstrasse in Berlin, seemed a suitable target. In addition, Lohmann had discovered that Phoebus had entered negotiations with American backers. The prospect of an American-controlled company in the immediate vicinity of his own office did not please him at all. But he realized also that the American threat would impress on his superiors the importance of his undertaking when he requested official aid.

At first things went well. The bank with which Lohmann entered into negotiations quickly agreed to lend 3,000,000 reichsmarks, provided the Treasury gave the requisite guarantee. By stressing the need to preserve the Phoebus concern from American monopolization, Lohmann hoped to persuade Dr. Gessler, then head of the Naval Department and Minister of Defense, and Dr. Reinhold, the Minister of Finance, to give a written guarantee.

Lohmann was not altogether happy about the date proposed by Reinhold for their discussion, and since he was free to suggest an alternative date, he asked me to calculate the good and bad days for the project. This request was entirely feasible; according to Indian astrological teaching, it is possible to establish the *Pakschachidra* days—*i.e.,* the days of inactivity, those on which specific enterprises are not likely to succeed. The fact that we were able to establish a favorable timetable in advance proved at least temporarily beneficial in Lohmann's case.

He succeeded in getting the money. But this loan was just the first step along the road that was to lead Phoebus Films deeper and deeper into debt. Just one year after the first massive injection of capital the company asked for more money to finance its big new production program. Lohmann not only believed in his idea, but he also believed that the films produced by Phoebus would enjoy a mounting success. He succeeded in arranging two further loans of 3,500,000 and 920,000 marks respectively, for which the state was again required to stand surety. That was in 1927. It was in connection with these new loans that I had my first actual meeting with Captain Lohmann. By then the treasury had guaranteed more than 6,000,000 marks for Phoebus. But before the year was out, it was apparent that Lohmann had miscalculated. Phoebus Films was a sick company teetering on the brink of ruin. By nature Lohmann was a cautious man. Why then had he not become suspicious of Phoebus' chief executive, Corell, at an earlier stage? Lohmann, in fact, was fascinated and even blinded by Corell's initial offer and his grandiose promise to produce films superior to *Battleship Potemkin*. As the project grew more and more fantastic, Corell grew more eloquent. He assured Lohmann that, once the films were distributed, the loans would quickly be repaid.

Not only were the loans not repaid, but they even failed to cover the production costs. In the end, mismanagement caused a halt in work on a feature film project, with many of the most important scenes still to be shot. At the end of 1927 Corell was obliged to advise Lohmann that unless still more money was forthcoming, the whole project would collapse. Lohmann had been tricked by the Phoebus management into believing he would have real control of the project. In fact, the actual contract gave him no power at all. Lohmann turned to me, but it was too late. Further investment would only delay the inevitable.

Lohmann had to face the consequences. In the summer of 1927 he was relieved of his post and sent on leave pending an official inquiry, and on December 7 of the same year he was informed that his appointment in the Intelligence Service would be terminated as of March 31, 1928. The official explanation said Lohmann had exceeded his powers. At this, Parliament and the parliamentary parties pricked up their ears, and the press began to report the great financial scandal. General Groener, the new Minister of Defense, did his best to explain that Lohmann had not acted dishonorably. In his speech to the Reichstag he said that Captain Lohmann had erred primarily because he had considered the Phoebus director, Corell, to be trustworthy and a competent film-maker. According to the report in the *Vossische*

*Zeitung* Groener said, "Even though the economic development of the Phoebus company failed to live up to the expectations placed in it, it should be borne in mind that Corell has now been made a member of the UFA management, which means that persons of authority in that great firm also had confidence in Corell's technical competence. . . ."

In other words, Corell had made a happy landing while Lohmann had been exposed and forced out of public life. His dismissal was nonetheless honorable, for it was stated unequivocally that he had at no time sought personal advantage from the Phoebus enterprise. And yet this affair was anything but harmless.

In actual fact the Phoebus Company was just one tiny component in the vast German intelligence system. Moreover, this investment, which had appeared so misguided at the time, actually paid off in the long run; the idea of shooting full-length feature films illustrating Prussian history was put into effect in the early 1930's, when the famous actor Otto Gebühr appeared in the *Fridericus Rex* series. These films used thousands of extras for battle scenes. In some cases the extras were regular soldiers from the Reichswehr, who were thus given the opportunity to take part in military exercises, albeit in historical uniforms. This idea had stemmed from Lohmann.

When film extras received military training and soldiers were disguised as film extras, it would seem that the film project launched by the Naval Department under Captain Lohmann had touched on matters which the Reichstag delegates, let alone the ordinary taxpayers, had not envisioned. Early in the 1920's the heads of the Reichswehr were already trying to circumvent the harsh provisions of the Treaty of Versailles by any means, legal or illegal. Under this treaty the German forces were restricted to 100,000 fighting men and were denied the use of battleships, submarines, heavy guns, tanks, and bombers. Allied commissions carried out inspections to ensure that the provisions were observed. But the heads of the Reichswehr were extremely adept at evading such restrictions. The regular army was highly trained, and work was carried out secretly—long before Hitler came to power—on the development of new weapons systems, some of which were probably even manufactured and tested. Germany also had an agreement with Russia, which remained in force for several years, whereby German officers were sent to work as inspectors for the Red Army and in the course of their duties, in which they instructed Russian soldiers, acquainted themselves with postwar developments in weapon techniques.

Although nobody knew when German rearmament would come, its theoretical basis was being worked out in complete detail. Battleships, seaplanes, mines, and torpedoes were designed, and special naval units tested their efficiency. Secret information on the military strength of foreign powers, on new inventions, and on technical improvements were collected and evaluated with great urgency. Further, the navy was creating fictitious firms, sham organizations which were used as covers for naval projects. For example, at Neustadt, on the Baltic, a sailing school had been set up, ostensibly to teach young people sailing and navigation. In fact, the "school" was training naval crews for a speedboat flotilla. Under the Treaty of Versailles, Germany was not allowed to own speedboats. Consequently, these speedboats were built by the Italians and "tested" on the Baltic. And, of course, the Naval Department was also running shipping concerns; it had a fleet of tankers on the Atlantic routes. Although these ships sailed under a private flag, they were available to the German Navy at a moment's notice. This was another enterprise in which Lohmann was intimately involved and when the Phoebus films affair came to a head, the Ministry of Defense, fearing further exposures, disposed of its fleet of tankers. Since the ministry had to act as quickly and quietly as possible, the ships were simply thrown onto the market, fetching far less than they were really worth.

Lohmann's hurried departure caused great confusion in the internal affairs of the Naval Department, as in the case of the sale of the oil tankers. A neutral Hamburg shipowner who was chosen to investigate the transactions and clarify the situation soon gave up. So too did Rear Admiral Oldekopp, when he was asked to prepare a full report on the case. Too many aspects of this complex affair were secret. Nameless subordinates had skillfully exploited the brief vacuum Lohmann's downfall had created.

The Naval Department ran other firms as well. The Bacon Company, for example, was a disguised naval supply depot which catered for the soldiers of the "Schwarzeñ Reichswehr." Finally there was the DEVELEV or Deutsche Velasquez Evaporato Studiengesellschaft GmbH, an international concern which was actually founded after the Phoebus scandal. This company—which was named after the Spaniard Velásquez who invented the evaporator used in the distillation of gasoline from crude petroleum—carried out technical experiments for military research. Influential civilians—e.g., bank directors, senators, judges, and industrialists—were of course also involved in these secret operations.

When Lohmann first found that he was getting into difficulties, he sent me the birth data of virtually all the important people working for him at that time, and I cast brief horoscopes of them for him. The copies are still in my files. To the contemporary reader these firms, which Lohmann ran in the late 1920's, may well seem fantastic. But they were anything but fantasies. A few years ago the Hamburg daily *Die Welt* published an article on the whole Lohmann affair. Commenting on the firms which Lohmann had founded, the correspondent wrote, "He was never able to give a credible explanation for them." Lohmann could have given that explanation, but he would have had to expose the whole network of German and foreign firms involved in these activities.

My connection with Lohmann brought me many astrological commissions, most of which had to be executed in a great hurry. I always received an appropriate fee for my services, and for the first time in my life I was able to maintain myself from my earnings as an astrologer. Still, Lohmann took up so much of my time that for weeks on end I was obliged to give up any other work. My astrological documents for the few years Lohmann was my client fill a row of box-files.

Walter Lohmann was a zealous supporter of the *ancien régime* in Germany, a man who had absolutely nothing in common with the fascist hooligans of the time. He was the exact opposite of Herbert Volck. But he was convinced that his manifold plans and activities would help restore the old social and political order. This may well have been his crucial weakness. He was a patriot who believed that Germany was destined to reenter the field of international politics and, once there, to play its part as a great military power. Consequently, it was not at all difficult for him to do what was required of him in his

capacity as a staff officer and head of intelligence: to promote the illegal rearmament of his country while camou-
flaging it from the inquisitive eyes of foreign agents.

Although the foreign press scarcely mentioned the
Phoebus scandal or Lohmann's dismissal, it was certainly
noted in other quarters abroad that Lohmann, a man
with such extensive connections, had become "available."
Lohmann did have many friends in foreign countries.
Lord Beaverbrook, for example, often invited him for
talks. At the end of October, 1928, an English industrial-
ist suddenly appeared in Berlin and offered Lohmann the
German agency rights for a new type of coal-dust fuel
which he had patented. This man, John Hamilton, had
worked with Lohmann immediately following the armistice, when they had both been engaged in the repatria-
tion of prisoners of war. He now offered him a livelihood
which would enable him to continue to exploit his foreign connections in the interests of the Naval Department. And this was just the first of many new enterprises
in which Lohmann became involved. Shortly afterward
he negotiated industrial and arms deals for a Swiss firm
and handled engineering patents in Italy, Spain, and the
Balkans. As a result of these activities, he acquired
knowledge of new technical developments which the
Naval Department found extremely useful.

Although no longer a member of the German intelligence service, Lohmann still felt a bond of loyalty and so
passed on any information which he received. The dangers in the life of an international trade representative
and lobbyist are sometimes just as great as those of the
head of an intelligence department. It was in Lohmann's
nature to become embroiled in strange adventures.

In 1929 Lohmann entered into negotiations with a

group of Italian financiers. Under discussion was the design, construction, and testing of very large military aircraft. Since it was proposed to employ German technicians on the construction work and since this was forbidden under the Treaty of Versailles, the project was to be passed off as a harmless commercial development program. A second project discussed at that time was the construction of two new fast steamers. The building contracts for these vessels were to be placed with the German yards by the Italian government.

On his way home from the initial negotiations in Milan, at the end of October, 1929, Lohmann wrote to me from Lugano, where he had broken off his journey to stay with relatives for reasons of safety, as well as health. Lohmann suspected that his mail was being opened, and so he corresponded with me by courier. In his letter he told me that he had conducted successful discussions with Mussolini and his Minister of Aviation, Balbo, on October 4, 5, and 6, 1929, the dates I had recommended in my electional chart.* The Italian government, he said, had found his project good in theory and, from a political and technical point of view, very good. But Mussolini wanted the necessary capital to be raised by private enterprise and asked that everything should be kept secret until the finances had been arranged. In Lohmann's next letter he wrote, "Berthold [in correspondence we always referred to Balbo as Berthold] is as interested as ever, if not more so, and sent me to see certain big financiers in Milan, Turin, and Genoa, with whom I am now negotiating; it is very hard going. I am due to report back to Mussolini

---

* A so-called electional horoscope is used to choose a propitious time for an undertaking. Electional astrology, very common in the seventeenth century, is rarely used today.

on the situation in Rome on Wednesday evening. . . ."
Subsequently, when I sent him his new horoscope for
1930, he remarked, "My horoscope is not exactly rosy!
The stomach trouble arrived on time to the day but has
now cleared up. . . . I am living in Rome, Hotel Majes-
tic." The airship company was floated shortly afterward.
Lohmann became the Italian representative of the
Schütte-Lanz works in Mannheim, a post which enabled
him to continue his political work—from behind the
scenes, of course—for the German Naval Department.

But then I heard that Lohmann's chief Italian associate, Signor Civelli, had died following a severe hemor-
rhage. Lohmann was deeply shocked. He wrote to me
from the Tyrol: "I am quite dispirited by the loss of this
man who was in charge of the airship project. Everything
seems to be going wrong. . . . I find no peace here and am
driven on by a feeling of restlessness." And so Lohmann
rushed from project to project.

Finally he tried to set up the Holland–Batavia Airline,
a tripartite venture among the Italians, the Germans, and
the Spanish, with the object of testing the large aircraft
then in course of development. It was a magnificent idea,
and it seemed now as if Lohmann, who had always had any
number of different plans going at the same time, had at
last succeeded in evolving a single, all-embracing project.
The Phoebus scandal had evidently done him little
harm; he was still regarded as a man of intelligence and
imagination. Mussolini wanted to use the first of the new
large aircraft for the nonstop transatlantic formation
flight. The technical arrangements for this project were
left to the Germans and—since Italy's financial resources
were limited—Holland was asked to provide the backing.
Hence the inoffensive and highly misleading name of the
Holland–Batavia Airline.

But after Civelli's death, it soon became apparent that the Italian Aviation Minister, Balbo, was virtually sabotaging the project. The reasons for this were no doubt largely personal. Lohmann had been asked by Mussolini to take charge of the production program for the new large aircraft and to organize the Atlantic crossing. The ambitious Balbo could not bear to see a former German officer preferred in this way. Relations between Balbo and Lohmann also appear to have been clouded by a beautiful woman who figured in our correspondence as Clara Maria Thirty-Three. She knew both Mussolini and Balbo very well and was also a friend of Lohmann's, who thought her reliable and trustworthy. In fact, she was neither. When she appeared on the scene, Lohmann entered on the last tragic phase of his turbulent and unhappy life.

I was first told about Clara Maria at a time when I myself was caught up in an extremely unpleasant situation. Volck's bomb trial had just started, and I was being subjected to malicious attacks in the daily press. Lohmann wrote to me, "I am told that my letters are reaching you without mishap. . . . That is a great relief. Please make sure that the names do not fall into the wrong hands." Our courier, Frau von Lerche-Igelstein, had already taken the necessary precautions.

Clara Maria Thirty-Three had a magnificently appointed salon in Rome and moved behind the scenes of Italian politics with the skill of a true vamp. Lohmann had asked me to compare both Clara Maria's and Balbo's horoscopes with his own. He told me Clara Maria's birthdate—she had been born prematurely in 1900, on a train traveling from Italy to Strasbourg. My analysis revealed catastrophic influences. At the end of April, 1930, Lohmann came to Hamburg for a personal consultation and was due to return to Rome the following day. When he left me, he said, "The way you have been warning me on this occasion, anyone would think this were my last journey!" I begged him to postpone his departure but to no avail. Frau von Lerche-Igelstein and another friend accompanied Lohmann to the station. On their way there he told them about his consultation: "This time Wulff spoke very strangely, 'You will never see Berlin again if you go to Rome now.' I suppose he is trying to prevent me from visiting these 'dangerous' people."

Lohmann went to Rome. As arranged, he met Clara Maria Thirty-Three in her splendid apartment and spent the night of April 29–30 with her. He did not live to see the morning—he had fallen into a trap set for him by Balbo. Clara Maria and her chauffeur are supposed to have brought him back to his hotel, where a doctor was called to where Lohmann lay in agony. All the doctor could do for him was establish the cause of death: heart failure. But the circumstances surrounding Lohmann's death were never cleared up. The plans and instructions for the transatlantic flight which he had brought with him had disappeared from his luggage. One thousand reichsmarks were found in his briefcase, but it was a known fact that on that particular day Lohmann had been carrying 30,000 reichsmarks. Twenty-nine thousand marks had vanished without trace, and Clara Maria Thirty-Three was soon being hunted by the Italian and German police.

Lohmann's wife went to Rome at once. When she asked to see her husband's body, she was handed a small casket containing his ashes. Somebody had ordered his immediate cremation; it seems likely that this was in order to wipe out traces of poison. Clara Maria, the probable culprit, had fled abroad. She had been Lohmann's agent, Balbo's accomplice, and Mussolini's friend. She had probably also been the mistress of all three. Although Captain Lohmann's plans had disappeared, Balbo was able to carry out the transatlantic flight shortly afterward and took all the credit for himself. But he was not to enjoy the fruits of his victory. When he heard of Lohmann's death, Mussolini launched a vigorous investigation which gradually shed light on the whole affair. Il Duce discovered that Clara Maria Thirty-Three had extended her "friendship" to Lohmann and Balbo, as well as to himself. Balbo was then relieved of his post as Minister of Aviation and posted to Tripoli as provincial governor.

Captain Lohmann's fate, which was so clearly outlined in his horoscope, bears out the dictum of an ancient Chinese sage: "The course of a man's life, once decreed by destiny, cannot be arrested by human calculations."

CHAPTER 4

# In the Hands of the Gestapo

At the time of Captain Lohmann's death the political situation in Germany was catastrophic, and the country was close to civil war. Not long afterward the Nazis were to take over completely. These circumstances had a profound effect on my astrological practice. In the early 1930's astrology was not so popular in Germany as it is today. But it had achieved a particularly high standard. An unbiased British expert who worked for the Secret Service after 1945, and so gained access to a large number of astrological studies discovered in the Gestapo files, has said that German astrology was supreme in the 1930's and that he could not understand why the Nazis had turned their backs on the qualified astrologers in their own country. The fact that prominent National Socialists like Rudolf Hess, Heinrich Himmler, and Walter Schellenberg—to name but a few—made use of astrology did not alter the official attitude. Soon after 1933 the astrologers in many German provinces were forbidden to practice. In other areas—for example, in my own hometown of Hamburg—the anti-astrology propaganda was enough to frighten the clients away. I have already mentioned that this new development created considerable financial difficulties for me. Virtually every one of my few "big" clients either went over to the other camp or kept away for fear of the political consequences, while my smaller clients were simply terrified. This left me with a number of Jewish clients, who were being subjected to even worse persecution than we astrologers. And so astrology acquired the aura of an esoteric doctrine. It was reduced to a trade which flourished in the underworld but which nobody dared mention in public. I was fortunate in that Prince Georg zu Sachsen-Meiningen, the father-in-law of Otto von Habsburg, still consulted me. He had quickly come to terms with the new government and, because of his social status, could afford to maintain his connection with me.

But these reversals were simply a foretaste of the great difficulties I was to face a few years later. The dark clouds then gathering on the German horizon were portents. Faced with the constant expansion of my astrological practice, I had virtually given up my artistic career, and now my new livelihood was also threatened. An astrologer is no medicine man. His knowledge and experience do not free him from the force of his own destiny. The fact that I was able to survive was due perhaps to my greater awareness of the problems and dangers which awaited me: arrest, the Fuhlsbüttel concentration camp, the Hartzwalde "branch" of Ravensbrück concentration camp, and, finally, Heinrich Himmler and his senior functionaries, for whom I was obliged to work under pain of death.

In June, 1941, one month after Hess' flight to Scotland, I, too, was caught in the Gestapo's net. Himmler's myrmidons liked to perform their duties at first light. I was lying awake when the Gestapo rang my bell between 3 and 4 A.M. When I opened the door, four Gestapo men rushed into my apartment, ransacked several rooms, tore books at random from their shelves, thumbed through my files and card indexes, and threw everything into disorder. I was ordered to dress and was taken at once to Fuhlsbüttel. At that time Fuhlsbüttel was a remand center, a penitentiary, and a concentration camp all in one. As the war developed, so Gestapo methods became less discriminating. I was subjected to the customary nerveracking interrogations. I was asked whether I knew certain people, whether I had ever cast mundane horoscopes (horoscopes of nations, groups, or movements rather than of individuals), and to what extent I was versed in the occult sciences.

The treatment meted out to me was anything but humane. There was no question of my being accorded the legal rights of a prisoner on remand. I was given no opportunity of consulting my lawyer and, like all the other prisoners, was put on a daily regimen of hard labor. But things soon changed when the guards discovered that I was an astrologer. While the other prisoners were clearing up bomb damage, I was taken aside and questioned about astrology. I sat among the bushes surrounded by SS men, many of whom made me look into their future.

As I have already pointed out, others persecuted under the Nazi regime suffered far more than I did. For this reason I do not propose to give a detailed account of my own experiences. But my spell in Fuhlsbüttel was pretty unpleasant. I was worn out by the interrogations and physically broken. I was also uncertain about the fate of my family. I had had to leave my wife, my daughter, and the younger of my two sons without any means of support; my elder son was serving in the army, and I had no news of him either. With things as they then were, it seemed improbable that the few clients I still had would keep faith with me, let alone do anything to help my wife. I was all the more surprised, therefore, when I subsequently learned that, immediately after my arrest, my wife had received assistance from several sources. In one instance an acquaintance of mine paid her a fee for a commission which I had never received. And so my family was saved from destitution. At the time, however, I did not know this, and the days and weeks passed in dreadful anxiety.

At the end of the four months I was released, as suddenly as I had been arrested. But I first had to swear that I would no longer work as an astrologer. I was also watched from that moment on.

When the gates of Fuhlsbüttel were opened for me in the late summer of 1941, I emerged into a strictly limited form of freedom. At the time I had no idea that the Gestapo, which had destroyed my livelihood and maltreated me, would soon be forcing me to work for them on orders from above. But, in fact, those very people who had forbidden me to follow my calling were to overwhelm me with commissions from the top SS leaders just a few months later. Meanwhile, however, I had other worries. I was not allowed to work as an astrologer, and as an opponent of the regime, I could hardly expect to receive commissions as a painter or sculptor. How was I to pay my way? I waited daily for a letter informing me that I was to report to some ammunition or armaments factory as an unskilled worker.

Shortly after my release from Fuhlsbüttel I received a visit from a former client of mine, the chemist and manufacturer Zimmermann. He offered me a refuge in his works at a modest wage. It was only later that I discovered that Zimmermann himself had engineered my release. He maintained close contact with the SS and so had considerable influence. Zimmermann's research department had been investigating the possibilities of milk irradiation and had developed a process that produced new substances in milk calculated to prevent the development of rickets. Zimmermann regarded this project as a real money-maker. But his endeavors to market irradiated milk for children had been constantly frustrated by his business rivals—often members of the pharmaceutical industry, who regarded this new method of his as a threat to their own products.

Now in a dictatorship, where the whole economy is subject to central control, the important thing is to obtain government approval and backing for any new projects, especially in wartime, when everything is rationed. It is distinctly possible that Zimmermann was hoping to promote his milk project by providing the SS leaders with some special treat. If so, I appear to have been the treat. What looked like the friendly act of a former client was probably part of a well-laid plan. The Gestapo knew that, as long I was in Zimmermann's charge, I was under constant surveillance. Conversely, Zimmermann could safely assume that by offering me employment he was doing the Gestapo a favor. And so, although I had no means of knowing it at the time, the position offered to me in the institute for milk irradiation was almost certainly a pretext. An entirely new and quite extraordinary phase of my life was about to begin.

In March, 1942, six months after my release from Fuhlsbüttel, I was instructed to leave Zimmermann's employ and proceed to an institute which I had never heard of in Berlin, to take up new duties as a scientific research assistant. I was recommended for this post by my friend, the Nuremberg astronomer and astrologer Dr. Wilhelm Hartmann.

I traveled to Berlin and reported to this institute, which was attached to naval headquarters. After the outbreak of war in 1939 research institutes had been set up for the army, the navy, and the Luftwaffe to test any suggestions or new inventions sent in by members of the public which might conceivably contribute to the war effort. In Berlin I learned, to my utter amazement, that the National Socialist leaders proposed to use these "research centers" to harness, not only natural, but also supernatural, forces. All intellectual, natural, and supernatural sources of power—from modern technology to medieval black magic, and from the teachings of Pythagoras to the Faustian pentagram incantation—were to be exploited in the interests of final victory.

The navy's research institute, whose activities were top secret, was run by a naval captain. This officer commanded a very strange company which included spiritualist mediums and sensitives, pendulum practitioners (dowsers who used a pendulum instead of a dowsing rod), students of Tattwa (an Indian pendulum theory), astrologers and astronomers, ballistics experts, and mathematicians.

The institute had been instructed by the headquarters' staff of Naval Command to pinpoint the position of enemy convoys at sea by means of pendulums and other supernatural devices, so that the German submarine flotillas could be certain of sinking them. Day in, day out, the pendulum practitioners squatted with their arms stretched out over nautical charts. The results were, of course, pitiful. Whatever one may think about occult phenomena, it was simply ridiculous to expect that an unknown world could be forcibly opened up in this dilettante fashion and exploited for military purposes. Even in those cases where there was some initial success, no attempt was made to evaluate the findings by systematic scientific procedures.

One of the employees of the institute was a retired architect from Salzburg by the name of Straniak, a refined old gentleman in his sixties who revealed a certain facility as a pendulum practitioner. He was convinced that his talent was genuine, and although he had the misfortune to be the author of a short book entitled *The Eighth Force of Nature,* he did not give the impression of being a charlatan. Straniak had claimed that if he were shown a photograph of a ship, he could pinpoint its position on a map. Officials from the Admiralty had visited him at Salzburg and shown him photographs of the *Bismarck* and the *Prinz Eugen.* Straniak had then established the positions of these two ships with the aid of his pendulum.

Many years before, Straniak had been persecuted by the Gestapo on account of his gifts. On that occasion he was packed off to the naval research institute in Berlin together with all his instruments and documents. The Naval Department, which lay behind this move, wanted to carry out certain tests. A Dr. Hartmann was then ordered to Berlin to check the movements of Straniak's pendulum for influences and deviations at sunrise, noon, and sunset and at the time of the full and the new moon. Other sensitives were also observed and tested at the same time.

Because Straniak was such an unusual case, a special experiment was devised for him: A small piece of metal was laid out for just a few seconds on a large sheet of paper. Straniak, who had been asked to leave the room during these preliminaries, was then brought back. There was no sign on the paper to indicate where the metal had been placed. But Straniak was able to pinpoint the spot time and time again and even did so from an adjoining room, using an identical piece of paper.

At this point the Institute for Research into Radiant Energy, in Berlin, which worked with strictly scientific methods, was asked to check the astonishing results obtained in the naval research institute. Not surprisingly the members of this scientifically oriented body were opposed to pendulum practitioners and all occult knowledge. The first investigation which they carried out resulted in fiasco for Straniak. For weeks on end he had produced excellent results; now he failed completely.

My own contact with the naval research institute coincided with the Japanese capture of Hong Kong. In this action Japanese soldiers blocked the loopholes of the enemy pillboxes with their bodies. Because of their complete disregard for their own lives, even the best-fortified parts of Hong Kong fell very quickly. At this point I was once again summoned to the research institute. As a student of the Vedanta and Buddhist Yoga I was told to submit proposals for the military training program which would enable the army to instill into German soldiers the Zen-Buddhist beliefs which inspired the Japanese.

Meanwhile, Straniak had fallen ill and was fast losing his powers. The other pendulum practitioners were in a similar plight, for their working day was extremely long and tiring. Gradually the members of the institute grew more and more nervous and irritable. Dr. Hartmann then suggested to the officer in charge of the institute that he should take his workers into a different environment.

Hartmann believed that the many disturbances and currents which pervaded the atmosphere in Berlin were frustrating the sensitives' endeavors. "Take your institute up into the mountains or to the sea," he said. "The sea air and the sunshine would do your people good, and they would work better." The officer followed his advice and in the early summer set out with his associates for the island of Sylt. In addition, working hours were reduced. But the results were even less successful than in Berlin.

Today it seems almost incredible that an institute of this kind could have been set up under the auspices of the Naval Command. In fact, the idea for this "research center" was not of Nazi origin. It went back to the plans evolved by my friend Walter Lohmann in the 1920's, when he was working in the Navy Office. It was learned after the war that other belligerent countries had set up similar institutes. Although no details have ever been published, it seems certain that England, the United States, Japan, and possibly the Soviet Union had centers of this kind.

Eventually Dr. Hartmann returned to his former post with the Luftwaffe, and I was once again placed in Zimmermann's "charge" in Hamburg, which at least meant that I was back home again. However, I was soon to be confronted with tasks which were even stranger and more dangerous and which were not so easily dismissed.

CHAPTER 5

# Felix Kersten

My acquaintance with Felix Kersten, one of the background figures in the dark morass of Nazi politics, brought me for the first time close to the Nazi high command. A great giant of a man who posed as a harmless masseur from Finland, Kersten had wormed his way into the highest aristocratic circles abroad and into the top strata of the Nazis. Although not an intellectual, he was a realistic and extremely shrewd thinker. He came from a farming family and in 1917 served for a short while as an officer in the Finnish Army, after which he fled to Germany to escape the Bolsheviks. Kersten then worked as a dishwasher, a film extra, a masseur, and—from 1930 on—as a "doctor of manipulative therapy." He was on Christian-name terms with the Prince Consort of Holland, Heinrich von Mecklenburg, and he was Himmler's personal physician.

When Zimmermann took me to see him one winter's evening in 1942, Kersten was living in a new and extremely elegant flat on the corner of the Rüdesheimer Platz in Berlin-Wilmersdorf. He owed these pompous surroundings to the "Aryanization" program, the former occupant, a Jew, having been evicted. The apartment was full of ostentatious elegance. The decor had been copied from the castles, palaces, and country houses of Kersten's wealthy patients. Our host greeted us sullenly. We had miscalculated our journey and arrived half an hour late. Kersten gravely told us that he was not accustomed to waiting for people requesting favors. He was entitled to regard our visit in this light: Zimmermann had told him of my fate, and from Zimmermann's sister, Gerda, he had learned about the irradiated milk project and the difficulties we encountered in getting it launched.

Soon the somber atmosphere which had made the first quarter of an hour of our visit so unpleasant was dispelled. Kersten's sullen mood lifted, and the conversation took a more lively turn. Zimmermann spoke of his concern for his milk project, and at first, Kersten feigned ignorance of the affair. Later on, however, he promised to help Zimmermann and to introduce him to the right people, who would use their influence on his behalf. Not long afterward this was duly done.

During the conversation I watched Kersten carefully. Was he to be taken seriously? At that moment he wore the look of an affable man, which is what Zimmermann had led me to expect. Greedy little eyes, which were reminiscent of a child's, peeped from Kersten's bloated face. He was a thyroid case and suffered from fatty degeneration of the heart. But despite his enormous girth, he was quick on his feet. His fat grasping hands, covered with small whitish scars, played continuously with a pencil or a little picture. In the terminology of medieval character assessment, he was a phlegmatic with a sanguine touch. He was extremely passionate and sensuous, extremely lazy, extremely vain and ambitious. Zimmermann knew all this and had correctly assumed that Kersten would be flattered to be introduced to an astrologer who might conceivably be of interest to Himmler. Suddenly Kersten said to me: "You can talk quite openly to me about political developments; I am quite well informed anyway, and I have my own ideas and worries about the war and the internal development of Germany. Now tell me what you think about Hitler's horoscope."

I very cautiously outlined the different constellations and drew his attention to some which were particularly bad. I then suggested that a man like Hitler could not be a successful national leader for long and said that I felt sorry for the German people; I foresaw bitter events which were bound to occur unless there was a radical change of policy. At that time the Moscow and Leningrad offensive had been broken off and our troops were engaged in "strategic" withdrawals which were actually to last three long years. I told Kersten that Hitler had the same Saturn position in his natal chart as Napoleon and that, although their destinies were not identical, there were certain parallels, applying primarily to Germany's Russian campaign and the battles still to come. I then suggested that if Germany were to be saved from complete disaster, something would have to be done soon. I did not say *what* had to be done, but Kersten knew what I meant.

Kersten then said, "Can you let me have Hitler's horoscope? I would like to show it to Himmler." I was terrified by this remark. Kersten saw my reaction and went on in patronizing tones: "My dear fellow, there's no need to be afraid. Himmler will not hurt you. I can arrange everything. But what you have been telling me about Hitler's future is important and interesting, and Himmler must be told about it."

"No," I replied. "I don't want that. Please don't say a word to Himmler. I don't want to be taken into 'protective custody' again by the Gestapo. Himmler must know nothing about it. He would not understand and would find my statements seditious. Please treat my observations about Hitler's horoscope as confidential, and don't make any trouble for me."

At this point Kersten asked me if I had suffered a great deal in protective custody; I replied that I had seen and suffered the same terrible things as other prisoners in the same situation. I then went on to say that my negative forecast for Hitler's personal future was borne out by mundane horoscopes, especially the horoscope for Germany and the chart for January 30, 1933—*i.e.*, for the founding of the Third Reich, which was supposed to last for a thousand years but which would soon be in its death agony.

"You must tell me more about this, Herr Wulff," Kersten said. "It is extraordinarily interesting and important for me and for the projects which I am pursuing. Now that you have started, you must go on."

Zimmermann also urged me to continue. He knew Kersten better than I did, for the Finn was an admirer of his sister, Dr. Gerda Zimmermann. But I once again declined. I told Kersten that I was unable to consult my documents because they had been confiscated, adding that the Gestapo had already discovered many of the predictions which I had made about Germany's future. All I could have told him then, I explained, were the few things I happened to have remembered. This would have given an incomplete picture, for some of my calculations and interpretations went back twenty years, and I had forgotten much that was relevant.

"You must meet Himmler," Kersten told me. "You'll like him. He is a nice man and can do a great deal for you if you want him to."

I refused this offer. I had no desire to meet Himmler in person. What I had heard about him was quite enough for me. Later Zimmermann told me that I was wrong about him, but Zimmermann did not know what I had seen in the natal chart. Kersten then asked me to cast a detailed horoscope for himself and also for Himmler. Himmler's constellations interested me as an astrologer, and I wanted to include his chart in the new collection I intended to make. And so I began to work for Kersten, but only after obtaining his assurance that I would not be subjected to further persecution at the hands of Himmler's Gestapo. A few weeks later I handed Kersten his detailed horoscope.

At that time I did not possess all of Himmler's birth data and so could not calculate a chart for him.

CHAPTER 6

# Find Mussolini!

My visit to Felix Kersten ushered in the most dramatic period of my life. It was not a drama of my own seeking. I was willfully involved in it by Zimmermann, who took me to Kersten because he wanted a favor from him and thought he could use me as a pawn. Kersten then exploited my astrological knowledge to make himself more interesting in the eyes of Himmler, Walter Schellenberg, and Arthur Nebe. His ploy was successful. Soon he was forwarding commissions to me straight from the head of the SS. As a result, I acquired a strange status. Legally I should have been in a concentration camp like other astrologers; officially I was an employee in Zimmermann's milk irradiation institute; in actual fact I was turning out astrological reports for the high command of the SS. My situation was undoubtedly better than life in a concentration camp, although the constant pressure of working at top speed on the most ridiculous commissions and having to produce infallible results was both trying and dangerous. I had no means of telling how long the SS would continue to patronize me as an astrologer or whether the slightest failure on my part would lead to further impris-

onment—or something worse. By the very nature of my
duties it was inevitable that I should know a great deal,
perhaps too much. And in dictatorships those who know
too much are usually unobtrusively removed.

I now entered a period during which I was frequently
collected from my Hamburg home by Gestapo men and
sent via either the Oranienburg or Ravensbrück concentration camps to Kersten's secluded estate at Hartzwalde.
A number of Jehovah's Witnesses—inmates of Ravensbrück—were working on this estate, which lay fifty miles
north of Oranienburg—*i.e.*, about one and a half hours'
drive from Berlin—and was a favorite meeting place for
the SS top brass. On July 28, 1943—shortly after the terrible air raid on Hamburg—I was standing on the road
outside my house loading some of my personal effects and
documents onto a truck for dispatch to Wohldorf, where
they were to be stored, when I saw two Gestapo officials,
Walter Wohlers and Meggi Mechlenberg, pull up on the
other side of the road. One of them called out to me,
"Thank God I've found you. I've been looking for you
for days. I have to take you along to the Gestapo post. A
telegram has arrived from the Reichsführer [Himm-
ler]."

As the two Gestapo officials took me to Berlin under
escort, my first thought was that I had been rearrested.
My wife and my younger son—my elder son was a soldier
in Russia—were again left in uncertainty. In fact, however, I was simply being seconded for special duties. Two
days earlier, on July 26, Benito Mussolini had been ab-
ducted. At the Berlin headquarters of the Kriminalpolizei I was brought before SS-Obergruppenführer Arthur
Nebe, who had been head of the Kriminalpolizei for
many years and now held the rank of general. He was one

of the best criminologists of all time, a master of detection techniques who was passionately interested in his work and would probably have held the same job under any regime. But when it came to discovering Mussolini's present whereabouts, conventional methods of detection proved futile.

Nebe's office was fitted out in the ill-conceived Renaissance style beloved of so many of the Nazi leaders because it satisfied their need for ostentation and display. Nebe received me in the gracious manner commonly used by detectives to soften up recalcitrant clients. He offered me Hennessy brandy and American cigarettes as if I were paying a friendly visit. Nebe then handed me the birth data of an alleged criminal and an alleged spy and asked me to work out a brief horoscope for each of them on the spot. I discussed the criminal first: "You don't need to bother too much about this man. He'll soon fall into the hands of the Kriminalpolizei and will come to a violent end." After looking at the information about the spy, I said, "This man has moderate gifts as a detective."

Nebe was noticeably shaken by these character assessments. Later I learned that the "criminal" was actually Nebe himself, and the "spy" was his assistant, Lobbe. Shortly afterward I calculated Nebe's horoscope in detail and gave a full report on it. The gloomy predictions which I made concerning the time and manner of his death were to be borne out by events. Nebe had been playing a dangerous double game for some time; he had close contacts with the German resistance. After July 20, 1944* he was obliged to disappear and was hunted for months on end by his own Kriminalpolizei. His amours proved his undoing. One of his girlfriends was forced to

* The assassination attempt on Hitler.

reveal his hiding place, and after being tried by a special court, Nebe was hanged on March 4, 1945, in a cruel and terrible way.*

But at our first meeting Nebe was chiefly interested in discovering where Mussolini was being kept. Indian astrology offers a method for making calculations of this kind. I myself had used it in a previous case in my practice. On the afternoon of the same day I was able to inform Nebe that Mussolini was somewhere to the southeast of Rome, not more than seventy-five miles from the capital. It turned out that this calculation was entirely accurate. Although he was later transferred to another island and finally hidden away on the Gran Sasso in the

* (In a letter to me dated May 8, 1963, Dr. Ernst Teichmann, a lawyer wrote:

"We two saw one another one evening in July, 1943, in the Reichskriminal-polizeiamt (RKPA) at the Werdscher Markt at Berlin. . . . The following day I learned that you were the well-known and respected astrologer Wulff. . . .

"A few weeks later the head of the Kriminalpolizei, Arthur Nebe, called me to his office. At that time I was his personal assistant. He handed me a detailed horoscope relating to a factory manager called Franz Schwarz and asked me to read it in his presence and tell him what I thought of it. Although basically a suspicious man, Nebe had such confidence in me that, unlike many of my colleagues, I could safely tell him the undiluted truth without fear. I saw at once from the birth data that the so-called factory manager Franz Schwarz was really Nebe himself. Among other things the first part of the horoscope provided a completely accurate although not particularly flattering account of Nebe's personal characteristics. Amused by this I exclaimed, 'But chief, you yourself are the factory manager and I am astonished to see how accurately the astrologer has characterized you!' To my horror Nebe turned pale and seemed quite shattered. He bellowed at me, 'Dammit, man, read the rest of it!' I was almost struck dumb by the grim prediction which followed and in which a professional and personal debacle, persecution, and a dreadful death were prophesied for 'Herr Franz Schwarz' in the near future. Nebe did not take his eyes off me as I tried to pooh-pooh the prophecy and pass it off with a joke. From that day on Nebe was frightened. Subsequently he became more and more nervous and was subject to severe depressions. I do not think I am mistaken in assuming that this psychological condition prompted his precipitate flight after the assassination attempt of July 20, 1944. You were the author of this horoscope!"

Abruzzi mountains, Mussolini had first been taken to the island of Ponza and was still there at the time when I made my calculation. The position of this island tallied exactly with the position which I had given.

That evening Nebe invited me to dine at the Kaiserhof Hotel, which had historical significance for the Nazi top brass because Hitler had been a frequent guest there before 1933. During the meal I had to explain Cromwell's, Wallenstein's, and Napoleon's horoscopes to Nebe. I drew his attention to the partial identity between these horoscopes and Hitler's. After this meeting I was allowed to return to Hamburg for a while. Shortly afterward Nebe sent me the birth data of twenty-five high-ranking Nazi officials whose horoscopes I was required to cast within a very short time. All these men were suspected of corruption. I was not told the names or the status of the persons concerned, although one of them, again, was Nebe himself. When I delivered these horoscopes to Nebe in Berlin—having been escorted there by Gestapo officials—I had an encounter with Himmler's adjutant Suchanek, who told me I had taken too long in completing my calculations. Suchanek said, "The Reichsführer has instructed me to inform you that you must work more quickly and take more trouble; otherwise you could end up like the alchemist Tausend, who is now in a concentration camp and will stay there until such time as he is able to make gold."

But my work for Nebe was fortunate for me. All the books and nearly all the documents which had been confiscated from me by the Gestapo in the spring of 1941 were returned to me on Nebe's instructions. He succeeded at once where Zimmerman and Kersten—for all their grand promises—had constantly failed. Of course,

Nebe did not do this out of the kindness of his heart. He wanted to get as much as he possibly could out of me, and so he returned the things I needed for my work. However, two boxes of valuable Indian manuscripts and translations were still missing, and later I discovered that Himmler himself had requisitioned these particular treasures, which were to play an important part in my first meeting with him. It was Himmler who later arranged for me to meet General Walter Schellenberg, one of his confidants. He did so partly so as not to lose sight of me but, more especially, to ensure that I did not work for Nebe's opponents in the SS command, which was then split into warring factions.

CHAPTER 7

# My First Meeting with
# Walter Schellenberg

I first met Walter Schellenberg, the officer in charge of counterespionage and head of Department VI in the Reich Central Security Office, in a Hamburg villa. It was an icy January day in 1944, the east wind whistling across the frozen Alster.

The head of Department VI, at thirty-four one of the youngest generals in the Third Reich, was a shy, almost insignificant figure. His quiet reserve made a welcome change from the brash arrogance of other high-ranking Nazi functionaries. He had a balanced physique. His head and body were well proportioned, his gait and gestures lively and brisk. He had small but extremely observant eyes.

Schellenberg took a seat a long way from the window in the furthermost corner of the room and immediately engaged me in conversation. His powers of deduction were apparent after only a few minutes. He was able to form a clear picture of people and events on the basis of just a few facts. I had the definite impression that this man with his highly analytical mind was not at all at ease in his beautiful and extremely elegant SS uniform.

Schellenberg soon brought the conversation around to astrology, and we discussed the constellations in his horoscope, which I had already analyzed. I told him that the period around 1909—in which he had been born—was astrologically extremely unfavorable: "Hostile constellations of Neptune, Saturn, Mars, Jupiter, Uranus, and the Sun were dominant then. What this symbolic, astrological language means," I explained, "is that there are bitter experiences in store for those born at that time. A remarkable number of such people have been deported and murdered or else have disappeared without trace. Others have become instruments of mass murder. If this uncanny fact were to be subjected to a statistical analysis, it would doubtless produce surprising results."

I then told Schellenberg that his health was suspect; he had been subject for a long time to great tension which threatened to exhaust his highly sensitive nature. As a result, his self-expression and self-confidence were often inhibited by excessive caution.

Schellenberg was not ignorant of the crimes and mistakes of his comrades and superiors. He was responsible for special counterespionage duties within the Reich Central Security Office, and he eventually inherited part of Heydrich's legacy. He achieved a measure of fame in German intelligence circles in connection with the abduction of two English agents—Best and Stevens—whom he lured across the Dutch border at Venlo in November, 1939.

Schellenberg was also engaged in highly dangerous intrigues with Ernst Kaltenbrunner, who was his nominal chief after Heydrich's assassination at Prague in June, 1942, and with his own colleague Heinrich Müller, head of the Gestapo. All three were intent on extending the sphere of influence of their respective departments, increasing their personal power, gaining the ear and confidence of Himmler, protecting their personal friends, destroying their personal enemies, and a thousand things besides. Being in charge of counterespionage, Schellenberg was better informed than most about the political and military situations of overseas powers and their attitudes to Hitler and Himmler. Behind the scenes he fought savage battles to prevent or to mitigate some of the enormities which were known to him. To what extent he was motivated by humanitarian feelings and to what extent by the desire to furnish himself with an alibi for future use, it is difficult to say.

At our first meeting such matters were touched upon only lightly. On that occasion Schellenberg clearly wanted only to question me about astrology; he said astrology was in bad repute, and he had serious doubts about many aspects of the subject. "Let us take an example," he said. "Suppose a railway accident is caused by a signalman forgetting to change the points. Now an astrologer will say that the accident was bound to occur at that particular moment because the constellations were such-and-such. I don't see that."

I explained that the sequence of events was actually of quite a different order. "In such a case," I said, "what really happens is that a certain constellation, which corresponds to a particular point on the earth's surface, triggers a whole chain of events within the cosmobiological system. A doctor might be inclined to explain the accident in terms of illness on the part of the signalman, while a psychologist, a chemist, or a meteorologist would explain it in other terms. But I explain it in terms of the specific constellation, which constitutes the outer husk of the corporate entity 'microcosm-macrocosm,' in which we are all enveloped. For the astrologer a constellation is simply the celestial counterpart to an event taking place at a specific point on the earth's surface."

Schellenberg then raised a further objection. "Astrologers," he argued, "commit a fundamental error. When they cast a horoscope, they base it on the moment of birth, which they regard as the beginning of life. But life really begins at the moment of conception. How do you explain that, Herr Wulff?"

This was another question frequently posed by intelligent laymen. "But a horoscope can be cast for *any* moment in a person's life," I replied. "We choose the moment of birth simply because it is the easiest factor to determine. And anyone will concede that it constitutes an important point in the biological course of a person's life. A horoscope based on this point embraces all earlier points and phases—the moment of conception, the growth of the germ cells in the parents, and even the line of ancestors—and also anticipates all the important biological processes and events which follow the moment of birth."

"But the moment of birth can be arbitrarily deferred either by surgical means or by the administration of medicines. It can also be brought on prematurely by an accident," he argued.

This is also a well-known objection. I explained that all such circumstances would be indicated in the horoscope by specific constellations and consequently would not be incompatible. The layman finds it all so strange and improbable, I said, because he is unable to see the intermediate links in the chain and because he has a false conception of time and space, one that is now being rectified by modern physics and by Einstein's theory of relativity.

"In that case," Schellenberg concluded, "astrology is an extremely interesting precursor of modern scientific thought. And yet it is nevertheless in bad repute."

I agreed with him. "The greatest enemies of astrology are astrologers," I said, "or rather the so-called astrologers—that is, the charlatans and newspaper quacks. But there are serious astrologers who are trying to bring the knowledge and the methods of traditional astrology into line with the natural sciences. Atomic physics is a good example."

Schellenberg saw the point at once. Then, with characteristic spontaneity, he suddenly posed a question of a quite different kind: "Do you consider that astrology is a suitable vehicle for the propagation of political concepts and for the political control of a nation?"

"Certainly," I replied, "it is possible to use astrology in the interests of the state, especially for propaganda purposes. The English did this on a large scale in the First World War. Lord Northcliffe, the famous propagandist, fully appreciated the significance of astrology as a means of influencing the masses. Of course, such practices can easily lead to abuse. It is questionable whether responsible astrologers would subscribe to them. Today our prominent and serious workers in this field have been imprisoned while the butchers and charlatans are allowed to carry on."

A few months later Schellenberg summoned me to his office and showed me a small astrological magazine called *Der Zenit*. Except in one small respect—namely, the addition of *Der* ("The")—it had the same title as the well-known monthly astrological journal *Zenit*, which was the official organ of the most important German astrological association until it had ceased publication in 1938.

"Here's an interesting publication," Schellenberg said. "It has been smuggled into Germany by sea from Sweden and turned up for the first time at Stettin not long ago. Subsequently we seized a number of wooden cases full of them. Dr. Korsch's name appears as publisher and editor but, as you know, he's been in a concentration camp since 1938.* What do you think of it?"

I skimmed through the bogus *Zenit*. It contained a good mundane horoscope for 1943, also the horoscopes of Admirals Doenitz and Raeder, plus the horoscopes of a number of German battleships. The latter were erected for the time of launching. I told Schellenberg that from an astrological point of view it was a first-class production and indicated that it was the work of experts. Some very skillful bits of propaganda had been casually inserted in an otherwise apparently innocuous text. We deduced that this fake had been manufactured in England, and I mentioned to Schellenberg that there were some very skilled astrologers there. Years later my friend Ellic Howe told me that he had been involved in the production of this pseudo-*Zenit* together with Sefton Delmer and the late Louis de Wohl. During my discussion with Schellenberg I told him about the bungled efforts of the Propaganda Ministry and our Foreign Office to use so-called occultism for psychological warfare purposes in France and many other European countries. I mentioned that Dr. Goebbels had been particularly interested in using the obscure rhymed prophecies of Nostradamus, the sixteenth-century French seer, for this purpose.

The Nostradamus "campaign" had been waged between the end of 1939 and the autumn of 1940. It had

---

* Korsch was already dead by this time.

mainly taken the form of sixteen-page booklets containing prophecies selected from Nostradamus by Krafft, the Swiss astrologer. Industrious writers in the Propaganda Ministry processed Krafft's "interpretations" to predict the downfall of the British Empire and the inevitable and total victory of Germany. The clumsy adulteration of the original prophecies and the obvious tendentiousness of the commentaries had been quickly noted in the countries where the pamphlets were distributed. One day the leading English, Swedish, and Spanish newspapers had carried the headline: WHO IS NOSTRADAMUS? A few days later they printed the answer: NOSTRADAMUS IS ADOLF HITLER!

Schellenberg was well aware of the spurious methods used by the Propaganda Ministry and the Foreign Office. After all, he himself ran an institute which served as a technical workshop for his espionage department, producing sophisticated forgeries with scientific techniques.

We moved on to the discussion of mundane astrology. Schellenberg, who was friendly with Kersten, knew that he could speak to me without reserve.

He told me in great agitation about his views on the ominous development of the Third Reich and the completely bungled political and military situation.

"Hitler ought to be removed, thrown out; only the concept of law can ensure the preservation of peace both at home and abroad. But such concepts are completely alien to him. It is very difficult for me, holding these views, to carry out my official duties in a conscientious manner," Schellenberg concluded.

"Unfortunately, Hitler's removal would not change the course of events," I replied. "Far too much has happened for that. I have been studying Hitler's horoscope for twenty years now. I have a pretty clear idea of what is ultimately in store for him. He will probably die under the hand of an assassin, certainly in 'Neptunian'—that is, enigmatic—circumstances, in which a woman will play a leading part. The world will probably never know the precise details of his death, for in Hitler's horoscope Neptune has long been in bad aspect to other planets. Moreover, Neptune is extremely strong in his horoscope, and it was always to be expected that his great military projects would have a dubious outcome.

"I have been racking my brains for some time now to see if there was anything that could be done," Schellenberg interposed. "Perhaps the fate of the German people might still be mitigated if it were possible to bring about a change in the government. Do you consider the constellation for Stalin and the Soviet Union to be favorable?"

"If the data which I have for Stalin's birth are accurate," I replied, "then he can expect a large number of highly favorable planetary directions in 1945–46. These do not indicate a Soviet defeat. But Stalin's birth data need to be checked. Could you find Stalin's precise time of birth, so that I can check my information?"

"I'll see what I can do," Schellenberg replied. "But what about the astrological prospects of Great Britain and the United States?"

"Much the same as the Soviet Union's! To put it bluntly, the constellations of these two nations are extremely advantageous right up to 1947. They reach a peak in mid-May, 1945. Action must be taken quickly if Germany is to be spared even greater misfortunes."

"Could you draw up a comprehensive report on all these questions for the Reichsführer?" Schellenberg asked. "I have found our conversation extremely illuminating and important both for my own plans and for those of the Reichsführer. I am very grateful to you for your candid account. And you know," he added, "what you told me about my own horoscope was absolutely true."

CHAPTER 8

# Lunch with Heinrich Himmler

One glorious sunny morning in spring I arrived in Berlin by the early train. Walter Schellenberg's private secretary was waiting for me at the station and drove me out to the Wannsee in a new Mercedes. We pulled up in front of a large villa. In the garden surrounding the villa beautiful old trees ran right down to the bank of the Wannsee.

I was introduced to a short, stocky little man, an associate of Schellenberg's. He and the secretary were to "look after me" and make the preparations for a journey to an unknown destination, which I was to undertake. Although he was not allowed to know who I was, I discovered that his name was Franz Göring. His colleagues in the department called him "little Göring." He was the sort of official who is always busy, always finding something to do. He wore civilian clothes, though he was, of course, a member of the SS.

Schellenberg sent Franz Göring to make the final arrangements for my journey. My first meeting with Heinrich Himmler was being well camouflaged.

The journey by special military train to "Bergwald"— the cover name for Himmler's quarters—passed without incident. At noon the next day, five hours late, I reached my destination. I had been told where I was going during the journey by the officer in charge of the SS courier railway coach; Salzburg was still covered by a smoke screen, because there had been an air raid there shortly before.

At Aigen, just outside Salzburg, there is a late-Baroque castle which Heinrich Himmler used as a retreat. He had it camouflaged and renamed it "Bergwald." This castle, with its fabulously beautiful old park, once belonged to Prince Schwarzenberg. It lies at the foot of the Gaisberg and has magnificent views of the Salzburg Alps and the Untersberg. Access is difficult, for the road is very narrow and full of sharp corners. We drove up hill and down dale along the zigzag route to the castle of Aigen, where our overelegant SS Mercedes limousine passed through cordons of SS and through the beautiful wrought iron gateway in the high outer wall of the castle fortifications. The driver gave a prearranged signal, and the guard allowed us to pass. I was admitted without even having to show my papers. But then for the past three days I had been cut off from the outside world and had been entirely in the hands of SS officers.

I was received by Obersturmbannführer Sanne and various officers on Himmler's personal staff and was taken, by mistake as it turned out, to the Österreichischer Hof Hotel. After refreshing myself and resting for a short while in my room, I received a telephone call from one of Himmler's adjutants, informing me that a car was waiting to take me to Himmler's headquarters. By the time I arrived lunch had just started. Himmler and his staff were already seated. But when I entered the dining room, Himmler quickly rose from the table and came to meet me. The cordiality of his welcome was so natural that anybody meeting him for the first time might well have been pleasantly surprised. Himmler placed me on his right. And so there I was, sitting side by side with the head of the SS, who spooned his soup and engaged me in interesting conversation.

Who was Himmler? A ruler? A man of steel? Or a political calculating machine? A robot with horn-rimmed glasses and a metal heart full of magical spells which had been put there by some evil genius?

In civilian life he had been a poultry dealer and manure salesman. The world had first taken note of him on June 30, 1934, in connection with the Röhm affair, when he had been obliged to order the execution of a group of "conspirators." Since then he had been known in anti-Nazi circles as the "bloodhound." Göring is said to have addressed him as a *Würstchen—i.e.,* an insignificant little man. Doenitz always referred to him as *der Himmler* ("that Himmler"), a phrase which served to conceal his contempt for the head of the SS. But what did anyone really know about Heinrich Himmler?

The large windows made the dining room agreeably bright, and after the mist had slowly cleared, the Alpine range offered a magnificent view. The plain, mountain ash furniture gave the room a soothing and pleasant atmosphere in marked contrast to the oppressive elegance and rich trappings of the dining room at the Horchner villa. The center of the room was taken up by a large oval table which seated about twelve people. On Himmler's left sat a young lady with sparkling blue eyes. Next to her was Kirrmayer, a former Kriminalpolizei official and an SS veteran. This ex-policeman was Himmler's "watchdog." He was completely unpolitical and fanatically loyal. His highly comic, broad Bavarian accent was entirely in keeping with his country manner. Kirrmayer was an elemental person, a coarse and brutal type whose square head bore witness to his ruthless determination and fanaticism. But I also detected latent qualities of friendliness and benevolence and the honesty and devotion of an old soldier who would have allowed himself to be flayed alive for Himmler. In choosing Kirrmayer as his watchdog Himmler seems to have been guided by a sound instinct and an unerring judgment.

On my right sat Obersturmbannführer Sanne, an authority on "race" and a student of Professor Wüst of Munich, the Sanskritologist and head of the "Atlantis" Research Institute. After Sanne came three good-looking SS officers, who glanced timidly across the table at their idol, the Reichsführer, but said nothing, even when the conversation at table had become quite lively and humorous. They listened attentively and from time to time looked at me with shy, wondering eyes, like children looking at Santa Claus. All three were immaculately dressed and their behavior was reserved, well mannered, and polite. Opposite me sat Dr. Rudolf Brandt, Himmler's adjutant and personal secretary (a head of department in the government service and an SS Standartenführer with the rank of colonel). His shortsighted eyes, magnified by his spectacles, watched me closely as Himmler, Kirrmayer, and Sanne conducted the conversation to which I contributed from time to time. Himmler's pallid complexion marked him out from the others at the table as a harassed man with onerous duties. Apart from him and Brandt the luncheon guests looked fresh, well fed, and healthy. While most of those present conversed freely and joined in the question-and-answer game which developed between Himmler and myself, and while the old veteran Kirrmayer with his large square head and his catlike jaw related current anecdotes and told of a recent "climb in the mountains with the girls," Dr. Brandt

looked across at me. His sad, serious eyes seemed to have
witnessed many terrible things. He was an idealist and a
loyal and devoted servant of Himmler. During the whole
of the meal and the ensuing afternoon this grave man did
not say a word. Next to Brandt sat two young ladies.
They were his secretaries and the last of the luncheon
guests.

The food was served by two servants in snow-white
jackets and gloves, who watched attentively but did not
speak.

Himmler was having one of his meatless days. That
suited me very well, for I am a vegetarian. My personal
philosophy, which inclines toward Buddhism and its cosmic approach, persuaded me at an early age that it is
wrong to eat anything that is connected with a tragedy.
Whenever possible, I have tried to put this idea into
practice. Himmler's motives were quite different. He had
gone over to a fatless and meatless diet because of a stomach and intestinal complaint.

In the plainly furnished, unostentatious dining room,
as we spoke of vegetarianism, Himmler told us that he
detested hunting because he could not bear to see an ani-
mal suffer. He waxed genuinely sentimental and assured
us that he could not stand even the sight of blood. Provi-
dence selects strange creatures as its bloodhounds and
hangmen. I have often thought about this sentimental
statement of Himmler's. He was agreeable and friendly
to his close relatives and is said to have been a solicitous
and loyal father. So is every bird of prey.

The fact that Himmler's watchdog had awful table
manners and behaved at the table like an ill-bred boor
surprised nobody. But such bad manners were incongruous in the head of the German Police, the Minister of the

Interior in the Third Reich, and the Reichsführer of the
SS. Yet Himmler was worse than Kirrmayer. He sat with
his elbows on the table and his arms spread out in front
of him, sucking his soup like a peasant. The Reichsführer
of the SS, Heinrich Himmler, made no attempt to conceal his lack of breeding, nor did his friend and faithful
guardian Kirrmayer. By comparison with the other
guests, who were all well mannered, they appeared positively grotesque. The young SS officers smiled furtively
across the table at me when they saw that the peasant
manners of their *Reichsheini* had attracted my attention
too long to pass unnoticed. Himmler then engaged me in
conversation:

"I am very grateful to you for coming and also for
having told Schellenberg about the *Arthasastra* [Manual
of Politics-Manual of Falsehood]. It is an incredibly valuable book, quite perfect in its way. The ancient Indians
were really thorough; they considered every important
aspect of government. I really am very grateful to you,
Herr Wulff. It is strange that none of my own people
should have drawn my attention to the existence of such
literature." For a moment I was speechless. Himmler was
talking about the Indian work which the Gestapo had
confiscated in my house and which Nebe had not returned to me.

When I had recovered I said, "Isn't it a marvelous
work? It contains all the wisdom that a statesman needs." I
went on to explain: "The ancient Indian world in which
Kautilya lived is completely alien to us. Internal order in
ancient India was based on a hierarchy headed by the
king and his advisers. Then came the castes, which were
strictly segregated from one another and whose organization and knowledge of archetypal images were very much

in line with the practices and concepts of ancient Indian astrology. Each one of these castes had its special privileges vis-à-vis the others. By observing their own particular duties, the caste members ascended to heaven and merged with the infinite (*parabrahman*). If this order of things were transgressed the whole world would be destroyed in the ensuing confusion. Further, in the Indian text we are told that man should 'apply himself to pleasure (*kama*) without coming into conflict with the morally good (*dharma*) and the useful (*artha*); he should not live without joy.' If one of these three—that is, the morally good, the useful, or the pleasurable aspects of life—is indulged in to excess, then the individual will harm himself and the two neglected aspects. But the useful aspect is of prime importance, for the *Arthasastra* was written with the king and the ruling caste in mind. The question as to whether moral considerations apply in a prince's decision is answered by the author of the *Arthasastra* when he says that what is useful (to the king) takes precedence (over *dharma* and *kama*)."

Himmler then began a long monologue on this subject. He reached a conclusion which was fundamentally different from that advanced in the *Arthasastra* and which surprised the nonmembers of the SS (in whose ranks I included myself). I knew that the *Arthasastra* imposed no restrictions on the king vis-à-vis his own people. On the contrary, a whole series of chapters is given over to the organization and functioning of an elaborate internal spy network. Now, in his remarks on Kautilya, whom he had avidly studied, Himmler described the use of such an internal network as indecent and unworthy of the Germanic people.

It sounds incredible coming from the man who had

built up a highly sophisticated and vigilant intelligence machine with such fanatical energy. But they were the very words used by the head of the Secret Police, by one of the leading members of the National Socialist Party. Although the party was a mass movement, that movement was composed of countless individual cells which were constantly being broken down and renewed. Every single party member became an "important link in the national community," which means that every party member spied on every other party member. Spying was omnipresent in the National Socialist movement; it extended from the meanest citizen to the head of the Gestapo, Heinrich Himmler. Acting on Hitler's behalf, Himmler organized modern methods of terror into a comprehensive system in which spying was the most important single factor. In everything they did the National Socialists revealed a marked preference for deceptive procedures. Lies and bluff flourished. Immorality thrived because it came naturally to men bent on terror. It often appeared as naked force, although in actual fact this force was simply a cover for conspiracy.

Himmler used the typical Nazi trick of advocating high ideals and qualities which he and his associates had never possessed. All National Socialist actions were undertaken in defense of a sacred, supradivine and, consequently, moral destiny. On that afternoon at the Bergwald, before an audience of his own followers who believed every word he said, Himmler was able to stick out his chest and wax indignant on the artifices and cunning openly advocated by Kautilya in the *Arthasastra*.

This hypocrite, this fanatical believer in the National Socialist racial laws and *Weltanschauung* (world picture), epitomized the cruelty and bestiality of the Hitler regime. Himmler laid claim to honesty because he didn't know what it was and to decency because he had grown cunning in the service of National Socialism. His SS methods were a perfect symbol of this totally immoral government. They appealed to the worst qualities in man: brutality, revenge, envy, excess, robbery, lies, and deception. The methods which Himmler condemned in the *Arthasastra* were the methods which he had introduced to Germany, where they triggered a degenerative process of such virulence within the nation that it was only a matter of time before it infected its instigators. In this talk Himmler described the unscrupulous actions of the SS as "sacred deeds" necessary for the preservation of the "Thousand Year Reich."

The maxims in Kautilya's *Arthasastra* were intended for a small Indian prince, whose territory bordered on the territories of many other princes. In all such states internal order was maintained by powers and forces which, although independent of the prince, supported him and were supported by him. That is why "usefulness" (*artha*) was so highly valued. The prince (or the ruling caste) had only one object in life—namely, to retain power for its own sake. Consequently the political problems of such a principality could be reduced to the single question: How do I keep my friends happy with sugarbread and how do I punish my enemies with the whip?

"For us politics means the government of the people in the fullest sense of the word," Himmler said. "It means the elimination of all forces except those serving the one constructive idea, which also determines our relations with other countries, even though this has been skillfully concealed by our foreign policy. Consequently we are not concerned with the individual but with the people, not with power as such but with power as the means of realizing a moral idea."

All this talk of "realizing a moral idea" was just so much soft soap for the masses. The whole fraudulent concept was designed to mislead the populace and gratify its need for "decency" by presenting it with a custom-made papier-mâché world. It was all a diversion, a philosophical brainwashing program for the credulous, who had failed to see through the swindles and lies of Hitler's elect. These poor dupes were to be exalted and conducted to what they fondly imagined was a higher and a "heroic" life in which they would bask in the "joy of the community."

Like all the top Nazi leaders, Himmler feared public discussion. And so he avoided my direct questions about the *Arthasastra* until we were alone together. As long as he was in the company of his little lieutenants, his secretaries, and his subordinates, he used emotive and threatening language and demanded enthusiasm for the "most monumental idea the world had ever seen." First he ranted; then he promised a better future, although the wartime years had already been extremely good for these Nazis. He also spoke of their great Führer's divine mission to his little people. It was clear that the audience at Himmler's table was highly susceptible to his words. Himmler used the same old propaganda devices which had been in vogue in 1933 and even earlier, in the 1920's, to charm his listeners.

After lunch an adjutant conducted me to Himmler's study. In the antechamber I was received by a markedly "Nordic" blonde, one of Himmler's secretaries, who then announced me. Himmler greeted me in the same effusive

manner as before. We sat down at a small circular table
which was ringed by easy chairs and stood in the corner
of the room farthest away from the beautiful big bay windows overlooking a splendid park. The skyline was
formed by the lilac-blue mountain chain of the Salzburg
Alps.

Himmler's study was large and spacious with little furniture. Here too the visitor was surprised by the simplicity of the decor; there was scarcely a single rug on the
parquet floor, and just a few pieces of modern furniture,
made from expensive, natural-colored wood and executed in Speer's Renaissance style,* were set out here and
there. Himmler's writing desk was simple. A small mono-
chrome carpet just covered the desk area. There was no
ostentation, no luxury. Himmler lived very simply. On
the wall facing the writing desk I noticed an oil painting
of an old Viking ship fighting against stormy seas on a
dangerous stretch of Norwegian cliff coast. This oil painting with its cheap theatrical coloring shone on the wall
with symbolic force: Himmler's ship of destiny sailing
past dangerous reefs in the stormy seas of National Socialist politics. The remaining walls in Himmler's study were
bare. The room looked terribly sober.

After we had sat down, Himmler rose again and hurriedly locked both of the doors leading to his study. He
then put the key in the side pocket of his uniform jacket.
He had already given orders that he was not to be dis-
turbed. His watchdog, Herr Kirrmayer, panted outside
the main door of the room.

Himmler briefly outlined his basic attitude to astrology and similar occult studies. His discourse was lively
and by no means uninteresting. He told me about a few

* Albert Speer was Hitler's "master builder."

of his own experiences and observations on certain phases of the moon. His ancestors, he said, had been familiar with peasant lore, calculating the right time to plant crops. Indeed he himself invariably began important projects at certain, but not generally known, phases of the moon. His speech, now that we were alone, was simple, uninhibited, and free from technical jargon.

"I am sorry that I had to have you imprisoned, but I simply had to put a stop to the public practice of astrology. In public it can no longer be tolerated. Everything connected with astrology had to be forbidden. It was causing a great deal of mischief. Frederick the Great also prohibited astrology during the Seven Years' War. He issued a warning to all fortune-tellers, astrologers, palmists, and pastors and threatened them with imprisonment if they said anything against the war and his policies. He advised the itinerant palmists to predict victories and a long life for his soldiers so that they would fight bravely and would not desert. He impressed on the pastors that they must preach from the pulpit on the holy and just war being fought by the Prussians and on their God-given cause. If they did not, they would be dealt with. The astrologers," Himmler concluded, "were also warned by Frederick the Second and were threatened with imprisonment if their predictions ran counter to his wishes and reasons of state."

"But Frederick the Great did not really prohibit the practice of astrology and the publication of astrological writings and calendars," I replied. "He allowed the people many freedoms. He was led by a sound instinct to employ the fortune-tellers in his own interests and in the interests of the state."

"In the Third Reich we have to forbid astrology,"

Himmler continued. "Those who contravene the new regulations must expect to be locked up in a concentration camp until the war is over. We cannot permit any astrologers to follow their calling except those who are working for us. In the National Socialist state astrology must remain a *privilegium singulorum*. It is not for the broad masses."

"I have felt the effects of your new regulations on my own body," I rejoined, "and I do not share your opinion."

"Did you suffer very much in the concentration camp?" Himmler asked. "Can you give me the names of any guards who treated you cruelly?"

"I'm afraid I can't," I replied. "I never knew the names of the majority of the SS guards with whom I came into contact. They called one another by their Christian names, and I have forgotten the few surnames I heard. At first I was very badly treated by your people, but later, when we had to work outside, clearing bomb debris, things improved. I finished up lying on the grass with the guards, interpreting their horoscopes."

Himmler laughed at this.

"You'll get nowhere with your prohibition," I said. "Those astrologers who have a good head for business are carrying on as before. They're just more cautious. Once it became generally known that you had banished the leading members of the profession from public life, the star-gazers began to make their rounds. They asked their prospective clients to give tea parties, which they then attended. Recently one of these star-gazers appeared at a wedding in Fürth, where she told the fortunes of most of the wedding guests, cast horoscopes, and was showered with gifts of money. The fortune-tellers are a little more cautious nowadays. Carried on in secret, without state control, this kind of astrology is very dangerous.

"The science of astrology is equated in your police regulations with fortune-telling. Paragraph Two of the regulations reads: 'For purposes of these police regulations fortune-telling is understood as the prediction of future events, the divination of the present or the past, and all other forms of revelation not based on natural processes of perception. It specifically includes the reading of cards, the casting of horoscopes, the explanation of the stars, and the interpretation of omens and dreams.' But astrology is based on natural processes of perception," I said.

"We base our attitude," Himmler replied, "on the fact that astrology, as a universalist doctrine, is diametrically opposed to our own philosophical view of the world. Astrologers claim to be able to cast horoscopes for the entire globe, for the whole of humanity. But it is precisely this that we National Socialists and SS members are obliged to reject out of hand. A doctrine which is meant to apply in equal measure to Negroes, Indians, Chinese, and Aryans is in crass opposition to our conception of the racial soul. Each one of the peoples I have named has its own specific racial soul, just as we have ours, and consequently no one doctrine can cover all cases."

"But in the astrological manuals of the Aryan Indians," I interposed, "constellations have been described which reflect the diversity of racial characteristics and which have found practical expression in the caste system of ancient Indian cultural life. Traditional astrologers have dealt with this problem in considerable detail from the days of antiquity onward." It was obvious that Himmler, though informed of the abuses by his police officials, knew nothing of the real achievements of genuine scientific astrology.

At this point he cut in:

"But the abuses among astrologers are very great, Herr Wulff. I know this from the police records. Astrologers have figured in a number of sensational trials. In Berlin this mischievous business of telling people's fortunes on the basis of so-called horoscopes had assumed such proportions in 1934 that I was already thinking of prohibiting astrology then. Horoscope shops sprang up like mushrooms in every corner of Greater Berlin and in many other big cities as well. Provided they paid, the credulous masses could discover 'all that the future holds in store.' That is fortune-telling!"

"The only pity is," I said, "that the serious astrologers were also affected by your ban when you cleaned up the bogus fortune-tellers in Berlin. The police ought really to have used this law to protect the public from exploitation and loss. But shortly after your ban was announced, when it was obvious that the police might launch a campaign against the occult profession at any moment, certain circles in Berlin founded a National Socialist Community for Members of the Occult Profession with the sole purpose of protecting those working in the occult sphere. At that time the Association of Scientific Astrologers, which was directed by Dr. Hubert Korsch and formed part of the German Astrological Center in Düsseldorf, was the only astrological body in existence. I know that the astrological charlatans have created a great deal of mischief. But so far there has been nothing to show that serious, scientific astrologers have had anything to do with such affairs or have been involved in sensational trials."

Himmler then looked through Stalin's and Churchill's horoscopes and went on to refer briefly to Hitler's horoscope. In my observations on Hitler's horoscope I had given an unvarnished account of the fatal outcome of his military ventures and had described his illness, the dangers attendant on his career, and his mysterious death.

"Hitler will not be assassinated," I told Himmler, altering slightly the interpretation I had given Schellenberg. "Don't count on that! There may well be an assassination attempt, but it will not cost him his life."

Himmler had already had my report on Hitler's horoscope for a full year. Herr Kersten had given it to him. In it I had stated that Hitler would meet his end in 1945. I had made a special point of stressing this fact in the hope of overcoming Himmler's well-known indecision and persuading him to move against Hitler before then, so as not to be caught up in the general debacle. I hoped that he would consider it necessary to overthrow Hitler and enter into peace negotiations or, failing this, that he would at least precipitate an internal revolt that would put an end to the Nazi regime.

"What do you think we should do?" Himmler asked. "Surely it's not too late to save the situation? We have reserve divisions in Russia which are still intact. Of course, they're not enough in themselves. We also have to secure the West." And Himmler started to talk about the "secret weapons," on which he set great store.

I expressed my doubts whether the new weapons could achieve a total breakthrough, outlined the general situation once again, and in conclusion, dared suggest that the only way in which Himmler could still save himself was by arresting Hitler.

Himmler replied without a moment's hesitation,

"That wouldn't be difficult. I could send Berger with a Panzer division and my men could take over all the other important posts."

This told me a great deal. Himmler really had anticipated the possibility of a revolt against Hitler and had even thought of leading it himself. "You know, Herr Wulff," he added with a hint of menace, "what we two are discussing is high treason and could cost us our lives if Hitler were to find out about our plans."

"I know that this task is difficult and dangerous," I replied. "But then any one of us could be killed in an air raid from one day to the next. I am convinced that foreign attitudes toward you would change, if you could make peace now and put an immediate end to the concentration camps. Hitler is so deluded he is past help. If things continue as they are, the war will soon be lost. That is why you must act! Your police force is still intact, and you can easily take over the government. For the immediate future your constellations are favorable and Hitler's are bad. Do not wait until it is too late!"

Himmler was pensive and downcast. "The only thing I am afraid of is the people," he said. "You know, this sort of action is not so simple. A take-over would trigger revolts in many parts of the Reich and also in the occupied territories, which I would have to put down with great severity. And there is no means of telling how the rest of the country would react. It is a very dangerous step, one that would cause serious disturbances." That was precisely what I was hoping for. Like my friend, Henry Goverts, and many of those in the Kreisauer circle—the resistance group that was to attempt to assassinate Hitler on July 20, 1944—I felt that after Hitler's downfall a "battle of the Diadochi" was inevitable and that this would result in the complete destruction of National Socialism.

"But at the worst the disturbances would be crushed within two to three months," I urged, "provided you secured the support of the leading generals beforehand."

"In that case we would have to act quickly. I'll think about it. Meanwhile, would you please . . ."

Yes, Heinrich Himmler was quite capable of saying "please" in a private conversation, when he was not playing the big shot.

By this time we had been talking for several hours, and I had had ample opportunity to observe Himmler.

He was a man of medium build. His abrupt movements suggested a nervous disposition. He spoke quickly and with lively gestures. He often made slips of the tongue. For example, on one occasion he spoke of a "nalivity" instead of a "nativity." This particular slip made me wonder whether Himmler had gone through my briefcase, which had been taken from me in the most courteous manner and placed in the cloakroom by an SS officer, because on one of the copies of my astrological reports the word "nativity" had been mistyped as "nalivity" and I had not corrected it.

Himmler's complexion was very pallid. His eyelids were red and appeared to have been inflamed by overstrenuous reading. The pupils of his eyes were mousegray and the whites so small as to be scarcely perceptible. His hair was dark, while his typically Mongolian eyebrows almost completely covered his eyes. His strongly domed forehead was not very high and did not slope away at the sides. On the contrary, his temples were puffed out and looked almost like growths. His chin receded sharply like the jaw of an amphibian or the mouth of a shark. He was badly shaven. There was a strong growth on his upper lip and his cheeks. His upper lip was pleasantly shaped, but the corners of his mouth were pinched and gave his face a sharp, cynical look, which overlaid his basic feebleness and cruelty.

I made three observations while we continued our discussion of the military and political situation. Himmler's views (it was the end of May, 1944!) were pretty naïve, and I wondered whether he was being open with me. He said that Germany would shortly make peace with the Western powers; England had been mauled and although the United States had not been weakened, it was not going to reach its full military potential. After an armistice had been declared and peace terms agreed with the Western powers, the war in the East would be continued. In view of the favorable strategic positions held by the German Army, the war in the East could be prosecuted for decades to come with the help of the Western allies. Had not Himmler heard about the Teheran agreement? Didn't he know that a separate peace was impossible? It gradually became clear to me that in political matters Himmler was an extremely naïve man. When I saw him at Hohenlychen, Harzwalde, and Lübeck shortly before the end of the war, this man, who held one of the highest political positions in the state, asked me the strangest and most infantile questions in his quest for astrological enlightenment about the military and political situation. God knows, Himmler was no genius. Rather, he was a mediocrity, especially when you saw him in private, unsupported by his splendid retinue.

After a short pause for refreshments, Himmler asked about his own horoscope. I had made a rough sketch of his natal chart as early as 1934. He did not know his exact moment of birth, and so, initially, all I had to go on was the planetary positions at noon. We now eagerly set about the task of establishing his precise moment of birth retroactively by means of "control data." In this procedure the astrologer casts a horoscope of the past and then checks it against the actual events of the subject's past life. When the constellations tally with the course of past events, he is then able to calculate the precise moment of birth and cast a horoscope for the future. While I was calculating this horoscope for Himmler, I noticed from our conversation and from his questions that he did know a good deal of astrology. He used a number of technical expressions which he had not learned from me. He spoke of trine aspects, of positive and negative signs, and of the elevation of planets.

As we sat together I passed him the portfolios containing my observations on mundane astrology. He became particularly engrossed in the report which I had drawn up for him on the question: "Is Another Mongol Invasion Imminent?" I complemented my written report by observing that the moment had probably now come for the "Battle by the Beech Tree," a hypothetical conflict which was prophesied by a centuries-old legend that developed in the Rhineland and Westphalia. I suggested that this battle, like the Battle on the Welser Haide, which also figured in ancient legends, was now imminent.

Himmler replied, "The Battle by the Beech Tree and the Battle at Untersberg on the Welser Haide, here in the vicinity of Aigen-Berchtesgaden, have nothing to do with the present war. They will take place in the distant future."

"I do not share your opinion," I said. "In view of the total destruction of Cologne—which is expressly mentioned in the prophecy—and the heavily bombed cities in the Rhineland and Westphalia, is it not reasonable to assume that the great Battle by the Beech Tree, which was foreseen in the prophecy and which is to decide the fate of Germany, has already begun? Aren't these events already upon us?"

Himmler did not take kindly to my suggestions. I sensed this and determined to be more cautious in future and to wait until I had gained his confidence by a few successful forecasts.

# CHAPTER 9

# Counterespionage Headquarters, Berlin

After the July 20 plot Himmler's position seemed, if anything, more solid than ever. By liquidating Röhm and his friends in June, 1934, ten years before, Heinrich Himmler had achieved a dual purpose: He had eradicated the SA as a possible rival of the SS, and he had proved his loyalty to Hitler. As soon as war was declared, Himmler had worked to increase the power of his organization. The expansion of the SS and especially of the Waffen-SS, which began in 1939, was pursued so methodically that by 1943 they comprised five armored divisions, four Panzergrenadier divisions, a corps of mountain troops, and a large number of formations recruited from the occupied territories. At the end of the war there were thirty-seven SS divisions in existence. Himmler's final objective was the creation of an SS-Luftwaffe. But this he failed to accomplish.

During the war the divisions of the Waffen-SS fought in genuine comradeship and with unusual heroism and fanaticism side by side with the regular army divisions. Himmler looked after his SS soldiers extremely well and —as far as equipment and replacements were concerned —they had a great advantage over the Wehrmacht troops, an advantage they fully justified by their sacrifices and high casualties. Although the differences between the Waffen-SS and the army became far less marked in the late phases of the war, initially the army divisions undoubtedly felt offended at being downgraded in this way.

When Himmler was made commander in chief of the replacement army and of all troops stationed in Germany, he fulfilled a great ambition, although he was anything but a general! In his new position he began to expand the Waffen-SS as fast as he could and with his Volksgrenadier divisions created a new kind of fighting force, which eventually developed into the Volkssturm (German Home Guard). But after Himmler's appointment as commander in chief, Bormann began to intrigue against him in Hitler's headquarters, although Himmler did not notice this at first. His units did not achieve a great deal in the war and soon started to run down. By the beginning of 1945, when Himmler had a nervous breakdown, they had come to a complete standstill.

I knew Himmler's history well, but the personality of the man was a mystery to me. Just before my first meeting with him I had spent some time at Hartzwalde with Kersten. I was full of dark premonitions, for I had long suspected that Himmler wanted to see me and that Schellenberg was arranging the meeting. While there I took a walk with Frau Kersten—a highly intelligent and agreeable woman—and asked her about Himmler. For a long while she was silent. Then she said, "It's difficult to say what he's like. He's an entertaining man, I suppose." After this she fell silent again.

But in the end the truth burst from her quite involuntarily: "Himmler's a swine, a real swine!" she said and told me that he had once made the wives of the Jehovah's Witnesses at Ravensbrück concentration camp parade in

the nude and then had them whipped. Afterward he had
walked away with a spiteful laugh.

Now my own first "audience" with Heinrich Himmler
was over. I had travelled to Aigen in a mixture of curiosity and dread, and I had survived the encounter. Schellenberg's fears that I might endanger myself and consequently him and the whole of the Kersten circle by
speaking too openly had proved groundless. I had the
impression that I had done rather well.

I had thought for a long time about how to deal with
Himmler, and in the end I managed to approach him
frankly and openly. It seemed to me at the time that I
had achieved my purpose: I had described the hopeless
political situation and Hitler's horoscope in the blackest
possible terms, I had urged him to stage a putsch, and yet
I had gained something approaching his confidence.

Once I was back in Berlin I drove straight to counterespionage headquarters in the Berkärstrasse in Dahlem to
report to Schellenberg. The counterespionage department occupied an enormous multistoried house built in
the "utility" style of 1930's architecture and surrounded
by chunky-looking bunkers, garages, and an enormous
courtyard. Schellenberg sat in the midst of the network of
endless corridors leading to the various subdepartments,
which were split up according to provinces and subjects
like a spider's web.

All visitors were closely watched by young SS officers
and were accompanied to the various departments by an
escort of two men. Anyone who stopped in the corridors
was automatically suspected of trying to listen at the office doors and was promptly shouted at. But, although ex-
aggerated, the security measures were really amateur. For
example, I noticed a number of sheds on a building site

opposite the entrance to the house which were not watched and from which anybody using a camera with a telescopic lens could easily have photographed every person entering or leaving the counterespionage building.

To reach Schellenberg's private office a visitor had to pass through two outer offices, one of which was occupied by his secretaries, the other by his adjutant, Dr. Schmitz. Schellenberg sat at a large writing desk with a polished top. On it stood a small attractive model cannon which he used as a paperweight. But on the left and right, within easy reach under the central drawer, special compartments containing automatic pistols had been fitted. Schellenberg had to reckon at all times with the possibility that Kaltenbrunner's or Müller's men might attempt to shoot him down. Next to his writing desk there was a switchboard that looked like a radio. It was used to control the bugging devices which had been mounted in the various reception and conference rooms and Lord knows where else. There was also a bugging device in Schellenberg's office. It was situated between the two windows and was crudely camouflaged to look like a cupboard. With this instrument he was able to record every conversation which he conducted with his guests. I found this extremely disturbing, and later, when I took to visiting Schellenberg more frequently, I always sat in the farthermost corner of the room in a small alcove, where I thought it least likely that microphones would have been planted. Counterespionage was equipped with every technical refinement of crime detection. The whole setup, which was both elaborate and naïve, was precisely what the man in the street imagines the intelligence service to be.

When Schellenberg saw me fit and well, he was greatly

relieved. He wanted to know all about my conversation with Himmler and, above all, about what I had said. I assured him that I had not worn my heart on my sleeve. "How long did the Reichsführer speak to you?" Schellenberg asked. I replied that I had been with him from about 2 P.M. until 7 P.M. "That's good, that's a good sign," Schellenberg exclaimed. "He doesn't often spend such a long time with anyone."

Schellenberg was well aware of the way things were going, and since he knew that Himmler was interested in astrology, he wanted to use me as a means of influencing him. He hoped that my mundane horoscopes would persuade the Reichsführer to have Hitler murdered and to end the war as soon as possible. Schellenberg had delivered my mundane horoscopes to Himmler in person and my own journey to Aigen—ostensibly to discuss the publication of an astrological magazine in Switzerland for propaganda purposes—was really intended to bring me into personal contact with Himmler so that I might bring a direct and lasting influence to bear on him.

At that time—May, 1944—Schellenberg was particularly nervous. The Allied invasion was expected any day, and Schellenberg also expected an attempt to be made on Hitler's life. For although I was ignorant of it then, it is now common knowledge that Schellenberg had been informed by his intelligence service and through his contacts with the Americans in Switzerland about the assassination plot. He knew Himmler was hesitating on the brink of removing Hitler, and he also knew that Kaltenbrunner was just waiting for an opportunity of eliminating Himmler. The more difficult Schellenberg's situation became, the more he came to rely on Kersten, Himmler's masseur and "father confessor," who did his best to ensure that Himmler listened to Schellenberg as often as possible. Kersten's daily contact with Himmler was an important channel of communication through which Schellenberg was able to pass information and slanted reports. Shortly after my return from Aigen the situation became even more critical. The long-awaited Allied invasion in Normandy began. Kersten came to me wringing his hands. "Himmler is still hesitating to act," he said. "He told me that his senior officers are no longer trustworthy and that consequently he cannot stage a putsch."

Things then moved quickly. On July 20, an attempt was made on Hitler's life, and Himmler, who had a guilty conscience, made amends by savagely and mercilessly pursuing the conspirators and their followers.

At this point Dr. Goverts returned from Switzerland, where he had been exploring the possibilities of launching the astrological journal. We had a talk in which I made no attempt to conceal my disappointment at the failure of the assassination attempt and Himmler's vacillation. It seemed to me that destiny could no longer be averted and that all my work had been in vain. I told Dr. Goverts that if it was at all possible, I wanted to get away from the SS. But he pointed out to me that it was very important to maintain this direct contact with one of the most powerful men in the Third Reich and that we must at all costs keep on trying to bring influence to bear or at least obtain valuable information for resistance groups. And so I was prevailed upon to continue playing the dangerous role of Himmler's astrological adviser to the bitter end.

# CHAPTER 10

# Himmler and July 20, 1944

Schellenberg's agents and intelligence officials informed Himmler beforehand—of that there can be no doubt—about the conspiracy to assassinate Hitler on July 20. Himmler's own plans for a putsch were then being discussed and checked against astrological calculations at Aigen. The conspirators worked in all the important departments; intelligence summaries of their activities were in Himmler's possession. At each new meeting with Schellenberg he received further information, which was then discussed. Himmler was extremely well informed, and in the astrological experiments which I conducted for him the questions of greatest concern to him were: "How will the Führer die? How long will he live?"

When I answered these questions and pointed out that Hitler would not die at the hands of an assassin, Himmler either pulled a wry face and grew serious or else sat with an expressionless, unctuous, bland smile on his face, which was quite out of keeping with his personality. But despite my warnings, Himmler chose to wait for an assassination attempt. His idea was that if such an attempt was made and Hitler was killed, then he would not have to go through with his own projected *coup d'état*, which had been discussed in April and May. With the intelligence summaries in his possession Himmler was able to play politics. As far as we were concerned, however, all this meant was that instead of taking action, he vacillated and continued to play his double game; he hesitated out of fear and so lost precious time.

After the unsuccessful attempt on Hitler's life of July 20, 1944, I was told by Dr. Goverts—who was in close contact with Gero von Gävernitz, an official on the staff of Allen Dulles at the Office for Strategic Services at Berne —that Polish Intelligence had known about Stauffenberg's plot on July 10, when it was asked to report on the reaction of the Polish and Ukrainian resistance movement in the event of a *coup d'état* in Germany. From this it followed that Schellenberg might well have been informed about the plot by other contacts as well. For the German opposition at that time this was a very important consideration. The fact was that Schellenberg and his department had had prior information concerning the projected putsch which they had not acted on. And since Schellenberg was an intimate friend of Himmler, it is inconceivable that he should not have discussed this matter with him.

Schellenberg had often complained to me about the lack of zeal displayed by his agents and the scantiness of their reports. Above all, he said, he lacked good, direct contacts with English and American politicians. On one such occasion I suggested to him that if he were agreeable, I could put him in touch with a reliable and suitable person who was in a position to make such contacts for him. It would not be difficult, I said, since the man's mother was an Englishwoman and was on friendly terms with the wife of one of the leading English politicians.

Schellenberg was enthusiastic and urged me to arrange an early meeting with this man, who was no other than my friend Dr. Henry Goverts. When I approached Goverts, he told me: "If my constellations are favorable, I will do it." His constellations were favorable! I then arranged the meeting between Schellenberg and Dr. Goverts. It seemed to me that the Hartzwalde estate was the most suitable place, because this would enable Goverts—who was anxious to discover whether the SS had had prior information concerning the assassination plot of July 20—to make contact with both Schellenberg and Felix Kersten. The private talk between Goverts and Schellenberg was engineered by Felix Kersten immediately after lunch on the day of our arrival. While conducting his numerous guests on a tour of the estate, Kersten suggested, as we were approaching the pigsties, that Schellenberg and Goverts should go on ahead since they had already seen the sties. On his walk through the Hartzwalde woods Dr. Goverts was informed that the SS had known nothing about Stauffenberg's assassination plot and had been taken completely by surprise. The contact between Schellenberg and Dr. Goverts became very close and cordial.

On July 22, two days after the assassination attempt, Felix Kersten telephoned me and passed on a number of urgent tasks from Himmler which had to be executed at once. They concerned Hitler's current state of health and the consequences of the assassination attempt. Kersten was so excited that his secretary had to finish the conversation for him. He wanted me to come to Hartzwalde immediately. Kersten was then living in fear of his life, for he too had been involved in the July 20 plot; the resistance leader Dr. Langbehn had been arrested before

July 20, and now his friend Wentzel von Teutschental had also been imprisoned by the Gestapo. As soon as he saw me, Kersten asked whether he himself was in danger and whether he ought not to return to Stockholm. I reminded him of my astrological forecast—he was in no danger whatsoever.

The evening before our meeting, on August 12, Kersten had returned from a visit to Himmler. "The Reichsführer himself has been placed in a very difficult position as a result of this assassination attempt," he said, "and wants you to check his horoscope for him. I shall be seeing him again in a few days time. He wants to know how this affair will turn out for him. And then you really must deal with my own horoscope in detail. This crazy business will get us all into trouble!"

After July 20, Himmler had had a temporary change of heart about his idea of a *coup d'état* because he was afraid of losing his position. But by the beginning of November, 1944, he was again pursuing his former plans, as is well illustrated by a commission which Dr. Henry Goverts received from Schellenberg.

Schellenberg asked to see Goverts again under the pretext of discussing the defense of Hamburg. After I had chosen a favorable day for Goverts, he traveled to Berlin accompanied by an SS Captain. This officer was not present at their talks, which Schellenberg preferred to conduct in private.

Schellenberg had contracted an inflammation of the lung and received Goverts from his bed, dressed in a blue-trimmed nightgown. Hamburg's military situation had been a pretext. Schellenberg referred immediately to Goverts' contacts with Gävernitz and Allen Dulles. He regarded the war as lost and wanted Goverts to arrange a meeting between Dulles and Himmler on a steamer in the middle of Lake Constance, in the hope of salvaging something from the wreck.

From the end of 1943 on no clear-thinking and un-prejudiced observer of the military and political situation in the Third Reich could fail to observe that Hitler was going to lose the war. At that time the German Army was desperately defending itself in Russia against the massive onslaught of the Soviet troops, after the Siberian divisions had been moved from the border of Manchuria. Hitler lost one battle after the other. Mussolini was finished by 1943, and although the Badoglio government was still being propped up by Hitler, it had no real authority of its own, and Fascist power in Italy was completely broken. But although the Italian troops were going over to the Allies in hordes, until such time as Rome passed into Allied hands, "Italy was occupied by the Germans," and Himmler was not prepared to admit that his splendid SS troops were being worsted time and again. During that period the people in Himmler's entourage were only allowed to speak of victory. Even the junior officers and NCO's received a directive to this effect.

Notwithstanding this ruling, the news which Schellenberg continually brought to Himmler was positively shattering. The invincible German Army was suffering one defeat after the other, and thousands and thousands of troops were falling into the hands of the Allies. From 1944 on German losses were counted in millions. The intelligence reports became more and more depressing, and after November 3, 1944, the tension was intolerable.

Goverts traveled to Switzerland to put out peace feelers.* In the Rom Inselhotel at Constance he conducted preliminary negotiations for the Himmler-Dulles meeting, which subsequently failed to materialize because Himmler once again backed out through fear for his personal safety.

Schellenberg's men—security officials—interrupted me in my astrological work with new tasks and insisted that I should give them priority. At that time I already had work in hand from Himmler—which was due on November 15 and which I had not even started.

During November Dr. Goverts needed to talk to me very often. Toward the end of the month it became clear that the military situation had grown incredibly confused. There were serious shortages of weapons and ammunition at the fronts. Gasoline supplies were cut, and there was, consequently, insufficient transport; railway cars had been destroyed en masse. The large reserves of stores which had been laid up in France—huge arsenals stretching all the way to the Somme—had fallen into the hands of the Allies, whose air forces had doubled by November, 1944. And all the time Schellenberg's emissaries and couriers were pressing for completion of the special astrological calculations for this complex political and military situation.

When we saw Berlin, we realized that one of the future projects planned by the German government—namely, the demolition of our big cities—would actually be completed before the war was over. The effects of this action were brought home to us in no uncertain terms. Unfor-

---

* He had already shown how good his contacts were on a previous occasion when he had brought back a Gestapo pass—which had been produced in England—for the ambitious Dr. Gisevius.

tunately the task was accomplished for the Nazi leaders by the Royal and U.S. Air Forces.

Kersten talked about the bombing: "What do you think they told me at headquarters, Herr Wulff, when they received the reports on the destruction in the residential quarters? They said that everything possible was being done to minimize the effects of the air raids and to protect the population: 'If at the present moment one or even several of our big cities should be destroyed, this would be regrettable but unavoidable and the population would have to bear their burden quietly and patiently.' Their 'present moment' has been going on for three years, but Himmler considers that the Germans are a strong and hardy race, who just don't care if fifteen or twenty million people lose their lives in this war."

He was right. The Hitler regime simply turned a blind eye to such considerations. "But what about the bombed cities in the West, Cologne, Bochum, and Stuttgart?" I asked. "What do they say about them at headquarters? How do they propose to make good the damage?"

"My dear Herr Wulff, you have no idea! The people at headquarters look upon Cologne as a hideous old city with dreadful old houses and narrow streets and obsolete public amenities. It doesn't matter at all if old Cologne is destroyed. Most of the buildings are worthless anyway, and after the war Cologne will be rebuilt—far better and far more beautiful—in accordance with the concepts of National Socialist culture and true to the spirit of our great Führer. These dirty, soot-laden old cities like Cologne and Düsseldorf can disappear from the face of the earth for all they care, my dear fellow. You cannot imagine the sort of things that are being said about the heavy raids on the big cities. Incidentally, they have exactly the same attitude toward Hamburg."

I then pointed out to him that Hamburg was not an ancient city like Cologne, Mainz, or Cassel. The major part of old Hamburg was burned down in 1842. Later, in the 1880's, the city was redeveloped and a number of splendid buildings were put up by wealthy old Hanseatic families. "These claims are both false and stupid," I said, "and merely demonstrate the ignorance of these men at headquarters of the city's history. The Mönckeberg-strasse, the Steinstrasse, the districts of Barmbek and Dulsberg, and many other parts of the city were new developments. Most of them have been destroyed, and since both Germany and Hamburg will be impoverished after the war, it seems unlikely that these districts will be rebuilt in their former splendor, with durable and costly materials. I am curious to know how the Nazis envisage postwar reconstruction."

We were driving through the Hohenzollerndamm district which consisted largely of new buildings that had nearly all been destroyed. Kersten said sadly, "No old houses, just trash! You know, according to the people at the Führer's headquarters, all the old buildings on the Hohenzollerndamm were just tasteless rubbish."

CHAPTER 11

# Count Bernadotte's Mission

Prior to December, 1944, Ditleff, the Swedish diplomatic representative at Berlin, had made repeated attempts to obtain the release of the Swedes, Danes, and Norwegians held prisoner in Germany. He and Count Bernadotte had tried with great pertinacity for months on end to establish contact with Himmler. But these attempts had always failed, because Himmler had studiously avoided this meeting, which could have placed him in a dangerous situation with Hitler. In January–February, 1945, a resolute attempt was made through official channels to introduce Count Bernadotte into the proposed negotiations. It was difficult for a diplomat to make contact with Heinrich Himmler or the National Socialist departments in charge of concentration camp prisoners. He had to apply through the Foreign Ministry. This was a long-drawn-out procedure and was unlikely to succeed. For a matter in which speed was essential it was, of course, totally unsuitable.

I was ordered to appear in Schellenberg's office on January 22, 1945. I arrived at 1:30 P.M., and among other things which had to be discussed and clarified, I was told of Count Bernadotte's mission. Schellenberg explained the situation: "Kersten is trying to put Bernadotte in touch with Himmler. Could you investigate this affair and let me know what is likely to come of it? I hope Bernadotte pushes things hard enough so that we can launch our old plan. It is high time. You know about the steps I've taken to date, but I can't bypass Himmler without exposing myself, so a meeting between Bernadotte and Himmler is important. We really must get things moving now." When Schellenberg discussed his plan for the removal of Hitler, he seldom made a direct reference to him. His aversion to Hitler was so great that he could hardly bear to say the Führer's name.

Kersten had heard about Bernadotte's mission in the middle of December. Schellenberg now told me that he had decided to establish relations with Bernadotte on a more or less official basis. While discussing a harmless exchange of prisoners with him, he could broach the all-important question of peace negotiations. Schellenberg also mentioned that Count Bernadotte had asked for a personal meeting with Himmler. If I were to give precise astrological information as to the possibility of a peace settlement, this vital issue would have to be dealt with first.

At that time the Yalta Conference was in full swing, the people of Berlin were preparing to defend their city, and in every part of Germany Volkssturm men were being mustered and armed for the defense of Hitler's "Thousand Year Reich."

Kersten had first started to push the Bernadotte affair with Himmler at the end of 1944, and during Kersten's absence abroad, Schellenberg had taken over, with the result that on February 17, 1945, they managed to arrange a meeting between Count Bernadotte and Kaltenbrunner at the Horchner villa on the Wannsee. On February 16, Bernadotte came to Germany, ostensibly to inspect Red Cross convoys, but in fact with the express purpose of establishing contact with Himmler. On February 19, two days after his talk with Kaltenbrunner, he was received by Schellenberg, with whom he discussed the projected meeting with Himmler. Count Bernadotte had traveled overland through Germany on his way to Berlin and had been able to see for himself that the Third Reich was entering its final phase.

After my conversation with Schellenberg one of his officials accompanied me to the Lehrter railway station, where I met Dr. Goverts, who had just returned from Stockholm. This was a fortunate meeting, for it meant that we were able to make the journey to Hamburg together and exchange news on the way.

The station was a scene of indescribable misery, made even worse by the bitter January weather. The entrance hall was completely blocked by refugees. The sick and wounded lay on the ground among the dying and waited until room could be found for them on the overcrowded trains. We managed to reach our places in our own train only by climbing in through the windows like young cavalry officers. The journey, like all journeys in those days, was sheer torture.

Goverts had not called on Schellenberg in Berlin because he preferred to discuss his news with me. In fact, neither of us was particularly interested in the course of events anymore. Because of Himmler's continual vacillation, the moment for action—for deposing Hitler and forming a new government—had been missed. The German people would soon be draining the bitter cup to its dregs.

In Hamburg we heard that Himmler was seriously ill.

At first it was said that he had influenza. His physician, Professor Gebhardt, was also ill. But Himmler had, in fact, suffered a nervous breakdown and was resting in Hohenlychen. His breakdown was rooted in his worsening relationship with Hitler.

Since the end of the year there had been considerable tension between Himmler and Hitler, which Martin Bormann had done his best to aggravate. Himmler was afraid of Bormann's intrigues and suspected that he was planning to overthrow him. And when SS Gruppenführer Hermann Fegelein, Himmler's liaison officer at Hitler's headquarters, married Eva Braun's sister—for purely practical considerations, of course—Himmler became very suspicious indeed. At that time hardly a week passed in which I was not plied with questions either by Dr. Rudolph Brandt or by Schellenberg about the discord between Himmler and Bormann. It was a full eighteen months since I had cast Bormann's horoscope, but now Himmler found it necessary to obtain detailed interpretations.

Originally relations between these two had been entirely cordial. But in 1943, when Himmler was appointed Minister of the Interior, a note of tension was introduced. Bormann scented a possible rival, and it was not long before sharp conflicts arose between these two Nazi satraps. As Hess' successor and leader of the party, Bormann had a great deal of influence with Hitler, and he soon succeeded in coming between the Führer and Himmler.

Himmler went in great fear of Bormann, and before every meeting with him, he asked me if there was any danger of his being arrested by his adversary. Bormann was the reason why Himmler decided not to reduce the strength of his bodyguard, even though extra soldiers were needed for military duties. A further stratagem devised by Bormann with the purpose of removing Himmler from Berlin and consequently from contact with Hitler was Himmler's appointment as general officer commanding the "Weichsel" army group on the Eastern Front. Although Bormann knew that the new army group was far too weak to resist the onslaught of the numerically superior Russian forces, he used their desperate but unavailing resistance as a means of convincing Hitler of Himmler's incompetence.

Himmler's simplicity of mind was amazing. Although he was afraid of Bormann, he failed entirely to see through his machinations. It never entered his head that Hitler might depose him. In fact, he remained firmly convinced of the Führer's loyalty until Doenitz was named as Hitler's successor. This too was a Bormann stratagem designed to keep Himmler's SS formations, many of which were still intact, at a safe distance. So long as he had access to Hitler, Himmler constituted a threat for Bormann. But after Doenitz's promotion, he was a spent force.

This left only Goebbels as a possible rival. And Bormann would not have hesitated to have Goebbels murdered if this should have proved necessary.

Himmler gradually became uneasy when news seeped through that ever since July 20 he had been suspected of having turned a blind eye on Colonel Stauffenberg's conspiracy. Bormann had engineered this "smear" in order to convince Hitler of Himmler's unreliability and incompetence.

At first Himmler refused to believe that Bormann could be so base, although he had long known from the latter's horoscope that he posed a definite threat. In fact, Bormann's hostile attitude ought really to have shown Himmler just how vulnerable his own position was and how necessary it was for him to implement his own plan of arresting Hitler's entire staff and negotiating an armistice. Now, following his failure on the Eastern Front, Himmler was laid up in Hohenlychen supposedly with influenza. In fact, he was completely shattered and wept ceaselessly. He asked Felix Kersten to come to him at once. But Kersten was far too preoccupied with his business deals in Stockholm even to think of hurrying to Himmler's side. Another four or five weeks passed before Kersten arrived with his "important plans for the fate of Germany," which he put to me as top priority. He tried to persuade me to accompany him to Himmler in the hope that I would help him with his selfish plans for business deals in Sweden. Kersten was no longer interested in negotiating an armistice. He had brought a long list of names of people whom he wanted to have liberated. Actually, the release of Swedish and Jewish prisoners had already been officially discussed—together with the question of the feasibility of an armistice—on February 19, when Schellenberg had received Count Bernadotte with Himmler's approval. Kersten's private aim was to win friends abroad to further his business plans.

CHAPTER 12

# Himmler at the End of His Tether

The past year had been nerve-racking; many of my friends had died, some of natural causes, others at the hands of the executioner. And the heaviest demands of all had yet to be made on me. To enable Himmler to contact me without delay, I was obliged to transfer a number of my instruments and books to what the Gestapo called my "temporary quarters" at Hartzwalde. My ephemerides, tables, and stellar chronometers, which were indispensable for my work, were housed in a room vacated by Frau Kersten upon her return to Stockholm. I was allocated this room because it contained the telephone switchboard with direct lines to Himmler and a number of important departments; these were privileges which had been granted to Kersten by the Reichsführer. Moreover, this room was particularly suitable for meetings and conferences. It also contained a small writing desk for me to work at.

On March 2, Kersten arrived in Berlin by air from Stockholm and traveled on to Hartzwalde. As soon as he arrived, I began a series of interpretations for Kersten in connection with his "worldwide political tasks." As he walked into the room, he said, "Yes, the fate of Germany now rests on my weak shoulders." I smiled at his remark. Himmler was still ill, and Kersten traveled daily in a car supplied by the motor transport department of Himmler's military command post to massage him at the hospital at Hohenlychen, which was run by Professor Gebhardt.

HIMMLER AT THE END OF HIS TETHER      141

While Kersten was away, I had to calculate and interpret his "problems" for him. Since I already had a large
number of difficult and delicate matters to work out for
Himmler, I found these additional tasks extremely dis-
ruptive. Moreover, when Kersten returned from his visits, he almost invariably inundated me with a whole host
of additional questions.

"Just check up and see how my talk with the Reichsführer is going to turn out tomorrow. Can I do that with
him? I just can't make him budge on this issue and don't
know what to do or what further arguments I can put to
him. He doesn't want to receive Bernadotte, but I want
to bring them together. And then I must make progress
with my own affairs, the ones I am negotiating for Herr
Hillel Storch. Just have a look and let me know how they
are likely to develop. Have you sorted out the other problems yet?" This was the way in which he greeted me virtually every day.

I then showed him my work and pointed out that there
were various special astrological reports to be completed
for Himmler which were due by March 10.

"Don't bother about the reports for the Reichsführer,"
Kersten replied. "He can wait. My affairs are more important. You must tell me exactly how I am to proceed.
Come up to my room for a moment and look at my horoscope. Herr Storch intends to visit Germany to discuss
the release of ten thousand Jews with Himmler. I have
already made the arrangements, but on this occasion
Himmler is being uncooperative."

Kersten had spoken to me about Herr Storch once before, and we had arranged to refer to him as "the bird"
should we ever discuss him on the telephone between
Stockholm and Hartzwalde. Kersten's statements and the

way in which he described his relationship to Storch indicated that this gentleman was determined to come to Germany to negotiate with Himmler in person, rather than work through Bernadotte. And so when Kersten arrived for the negotiations on April 19 and found a small and very unassuming Jewish gentleman, who looked about him with frightened eyes and was introduced to us as Herr Masur, who was representing Herr Storch, we were more than a little surprised.

Kersten always spoke of Herr Storch with great respect: "He is a very big man, the most important man in the Zionist movement and in the World Jewish Congress. He will be bigger still when he goes to America, which he intends to do in the near future. Herr Wulff, you simply must meet this man. He is going to launch me in America; I want to open a practice there after the war. I need Hillel Storch to get into important circles. My dear Wulff, why don't you come with me? You'll make a lot of money there. We'll go into partnership. I tell you, I won't let you cast a horoscope in America for less than five thousand dollars. If the deal with Herr Storch works out, I'll be somebody. You want to earn money, don't you? You don't have to tell the Americans the truth when you cast their horoscopes. Tell them what they want to hear, that's the main thing, and make sure you're well paid."

My relationship with Kersten was by no means as friendly as he was trying to make out. But since I was a concentration camp detainee working under orders from Himmler, it goes without saying that I was unable to give Kersten the kind of answer I would have liked. So I contented myself with saying, "Herr Kersten, let's wait and see what happens. We can discuss the matter when the war is over."

From my knowledge of Kersten I assumed that he was trying to make me more pliant in the hope that I would help him with the projects which he intended to submit to Himmler. I knew that he had no intention of taking me to America. He nonetheless continued to talk about it:

"You need only say the word. When I return to Stockholm, I'll tell Herr Storch what we intend to do. He'll get us passports now, for any country in the world. I can arrange all this for you."

"I hope they're not false passports, Herr Kersten," I said. "With all due respect to Herr Storch, I cannot believe that he is so powerful that he can obtain passports for any country in the world. Either the passports cost a lot of money or else we would be interned the moment we set foot in our new land. How can Herr Storch procure valid passports for each and every country? What sort of price does one have to pay for such privileges?"

Kersten replied, "For the time being you need pay nothing. Later, when everything has been arranged, some form of recompense can be worked out."

That is precisely what I had envisaged. "My dear Herr Kersten," I said, "I find transactions of this kind most uncongenial."

"But, Herr Wulff," Kersten protested, "there is absolutely nothing to worry about. I know how to obtain the necessary documents. You need fear no unpleasantness for yourself or your family."

"I would still like to think about it, Herr Kersten," I replied. "I will let you have my decision in a week's time."

"I can understand your caution," Kersten said. "But let me explain how it works. There's nothing to it really.

And, anyway, we know one another so well that there's no need for me to be secretive. If that were the case, you could hardly advise me. And you have always advised me very well."

I raised my hand to cut off his hymn of praise, and he continued with his explanation: "It's like this. Herr Storch has lots of passports in his office, mostly for South and Central American countries like Haiti. They are all perfectly genuine and are obtained from the countries concerned. Naturally, somebody with access to the passport departments must have stolen them in the first instance. But they all have numbers, and the signatures and endorsements are completely genuine. The numbers are recorded so that subsequently the authorities will know that these passports were issued by Herr Storch's office. This will ensure that they are recognized as valid. Perhaps Herr Storch has some sort of agreement with these countries. I wouldn't know about that. But believe me, Herr Wulff, you can rely on Herr Storch. If you want me to, I can arrange everything immediately."*

I still suspected that Kersten was trying to trick me into serving as his personal slave overseas. My experiences during the past two years had led to this suspicion, for Kersten had kept me fully occupied with unpaid work. "Herr Kersten," I said, "you will realize that I must think about this grave step."

Before he left for Stockholm, I thanked him for his offer—and declined.

Meanwhile, Kersten had been in Germany for a week, looking after Himmler. Today of course we know from

---

* A large number of such passports were issued at that time; Kersten's secretary kept a list of them. Schellenberg's officials in Department VI also knew that Kersten was able to procure passports.

his own book *The Kersten Memoirs, 1940–45* that Himmler's welfare was simply a pretext and that he had really returned on his own account, for what he called humanitarian reasons! The precise nature of Kersten's "humanity" and the personal interests which it was intended to promote soon became apparent.

Ever since the beginning of 1943, Schellenberg, Goverts, and I had been working for Hitler's downfall and had hoped to persuade Himmler to enter into peace negotiations with the Allies, release all concentration camp inmates, and repatriate all foreign prisoners. Without this token of goodwill an armistice would, of course, have been impossible. We knew that Hitler would not and could not make peace. His motto, with which the great majority of the German people disagreed, was: Conquer or perish!

Himmler had known about our plans since the beginning of 1944, and in May of that year, when he had consulted me on astrological matters, we had discussed their implementation for hours on end. For years thousands of Germans had fought or been imprisoned and subjected to fearful torture in Gestapo cellars for this same idea. Generals had sacrificed their lives in order to overthrow Hitler.

And now, at the beginning of March, 1945, Herr Kersten had appeared with his ridiculous list of a few thousand names and another "special" list (which contained just a few names) in the hope of averting the "worst consequences" in the name of humanity. It was unnecessary for a Herr Kersten to undertake such a mission. Action had already been taken in this sphere and had unfortunately already claimed many victims. But Kersten's mission was backed in the first instance by the Swedish government, which wanted to liberate Scandinavian prisoners. The interests of the World Jewish Congress came at a later stage.

Because of Himmler's hesitation and his reluctance to stage a *coup d'état*, the position of the concentration camp inmates was daily becoming more desperate. Hitler's orders—which were passed on by Martin Bormann —were that all the prisoners were to be killed and the camps blown up, orders which fortunately could no longer be executed because of the military situation. The efforts of the Swiss Red Cross to obtain the release of Jews and other prisoners, which had begun earlier in the war, were still being continued in 1945, although by that time they were of course greatly hampered by the worsening conditions within Germany.

After submitting his list to Himmler, Kersten had tried again and again to obtain his approval. But by March 10 he had still made no headway at all. Himmler was not prepared to release such a large number of prisoners because it was bound to arouse comment and might well come to Hitler's notice. Later he authorized the release of individual prisoners and in the end agreed to a figure of 1,800. But he refused to sanction the tens of thousands which Kersten had asked for on behalf of Hillel Storch.

Even after Himmler had given permission for certain prisoners to proceed to Sweden, there were still considerable difficulties. Disease had again broken out in the concentration camps, and many of those in the Eastern provinces had been evacuated. The transport situation was desperate. There was an acute shortage of motorized vehicles, and rail transport was out of the question because of the severe inroads made on the rolling stock by enemy action. The seriousness of the situation was made apparent to me in a conversation which I had with Dr. Brandt.

"How am I to arrange transport for so many prisoners?" he said. "We need all our trucks for military purposes. We haven't even enough transport to supply food to the camps. People just issue orders. Not a day passes without my receiving senseless orders from someone. In many cases we simply do not know where to locate these prisoners who are due for release. We lost all control months ago." In view of these difficulties, Sweden had offered, at the end of 1944, to provide transport for several thousand Poles, Belgians, Frenchmen, etc.

On March 10, Kersten, who had returned from Hohenlychen, came to my room and said that Himmler wished me to report to him the next day for a consultation. Since it was too early to assess the outcome of the last batch of astrological reports, I was led to assume that Schellenberg, whom I hadn't seen for a month, had arranged this meeting. In this I was wrong, although it was not until the following day that I discovered my mistake. At ten o'clock the next morning we left Hartzwalde in a Volkswagen which had been sent from Himmler's headquarters. Our route—via Menz, Fürstenberg, and Ravensbrück—took us through what was virtually a forward area. Long columns of refugees passed us moving westward, while the carcasses of dead horses and makeshift crosses with inscriptions recording the lives of children and old people who had frozen to death signposted the road to the east.

When we left Hartzwalde, a fine rain started to fall which enveloped the countryside in a gray mist. But soon the weather cleared and the sun broke through, gilding the quiet lakes and fields of Brandenburg. By then the thaw was well under way, and our route often appeared impassable. Beyond Menz the road become worse and worse; deep gullies, mounds of earth, potholes, and damaged vehicles hindered us and made our journey extremely difficult. But our old Volkswagen, which had been pretty badly battered in the war, got through. A few miles before Hohenlychen the roads improved.

It was only when we were on our way to Hohenlychen that I discovered that this visit had been negotiated not by Schellenberg but by Kersten. I was extremely surprised by the instructions which he gave me for our discussion with Himmler. I, for my part, intended to hand Himmler various astrological reports requested by Schellenberg, including a new mundane horoscope for the year 1945, and then to discuss once again the desirability of overthrowing Hitler and arranging an immediate surrender.

While he was giving me his instructions, Kersten appeared nervous. "But, my dear fellow," he said, "you must use the new horoscope to convince Himmler that my negotiations with Hillel Storch are important for him. You must support my project so that I can win Himmler around and get a written undertaking from him, which I can give to Hillel Storch in Stockholm." Previously Kersten's deceit and adroitness had usually succeeded in getting his plans through, for Himmler, like most frightened people, when they are ill, had to cling to somebody, and he chose his masseur. But although Himmler was very distressed at that time, Kersten had been unable to exploit his condition in order to further his plans for the liberation of Jewish prisoners on any really large scale. Himmler so far had granted only trivial concessions and authorized the release of just a few prisoners.

Meanwhile, Kersten continued to harangue me: "You can easily tell Himmler that it is written in his horoscope that he should release the Jews so that Herr Storch, a very powerful man, can obtain concessions for him from the Swedes and the Allies. A Jew is prepared to plead for Himmler! That's how you must put it to him! And if he gives me the necessary authorizations today, we two will share a bottle of champagne this evening and work through the other plans tomorrow." It seemed that Kersten had turned a completely deaf ear to Dr. Brandt's recent statements to the effect that Germany's transport situation was far too bad to permit the evacuation of large numbers of people and that, with the best will in the world, even Himmler could not provide transport for more than a few small groups.

"Why don't you try to persuade Himmler to put an end to the whole rotten business?" I asked. "The air raids, which have claimed countless victims and brought great misery to the German people, would then cease and the concentration camps would be automatically opened up. Himmler has been aware of Germany's plight for the past two years. Why don't you try to convince him of the need for a *coup d'état?*"

Kersten then became very agitated, repeatedly urging me to get his own plan accepted before discussing these other projects with Himmler. But I was not at all interested in helping Kersten, especially since I would have had to falsify Himmler's horoscope. As I saw it, it was not simply a question of helping the Jews. What was needed was an end to this whole senseless war, in which so many people were still being slaughtered. "My dear Herr Kersten," I said, "I shall interpret Himmler's horoscope in accordance with astrological practice." I then asked,

"Does Schellenberg know about this project?" Schellenberg knew nothing about it. The visit to Himmler was Kersten's idea!

Later, when I told Schellenberg about this enterprise, all he said was, "So our fat friend has been up to his tricks again!" Kersten's demands really were outrageous. But although I had no intention of binding myself, I eventually agreed to help him with his mission for Hillel Storch in some small way.

The questions with which Kersten had constantly plied me during the past few days at Hartzwalde and the investigations and calculations which these had necessitated were far more than a practicing astrologer expects from a single client; it had been sheer drudgery. As a result, I had decided that as soon as I returned from Hohenlychen, I would contrive to leave Hartzwalde as soon as possible and would inform Schellenberg of my decision after my arrival in Hamburg. All I had to do was find some plausible pretext. At that particular moment, however, there was no suitable argument that I could have advanced. I wondered if I should plead illness.

The nearer we came to Hohenlychen, the more the tension grew. Eventually we passed through military checkpoints and an iron gateway into a sort of park containing isolated groups of small buildings. Our passes were inspected by the SS guard. Kersten, who was a well-known figure, greeted the men at the guardpost with a jovial "Good morning to you" and not with "Heil Hitler"! We then drove along gravel paths to an open space, where we parked. Everything was spick and span. On one side of the parking lot stood rows of cars; on the other a motorcycle detachment had left its machines. When we arrived, we found Kirrmayer waiting for us at the top of a small flight of steps leading up to the first-floor level of a detached house, which served as Himmler's temporary residence. The house was closely guarded on all four sides by Kirrmayer's men. As usual, Kersten greeted Kirrmayer in a friendly and jovial fashion. I merely nodded to him. We were shown into a guardroom and asked to wait.

At last the door opened and a short, stocky, and rather corpulent man with deepset eyes entered the room. Kersten greeted him coolly and then introduced me. This man was SS Obergruppenführer Professor Gebhardt, Himmler's physician, who looked at us inquisitively before asking us to go into the adjoining room.* We found ourselves in Himmler's sitting room, a small room, its French windows leading to a balcony which I had noticed from the outside when we were entering the house.

Heinrich Himmler was seated in an easy chair and asked me to sit beside him. He had just woken and smelled of soap and cheap cologne; his complexion was fresher than usual, and he seemed to have made a reasonable recovery. Kersten's treatment had evidently helped. The masseur meanwhile had made himself comfortable on an old-fashioned sofa. Simple curtains made of beige and brown muslin with a red and green pattern hung on either side of the French windows. An old-fashioned lamp hung from the ceiling; it had a shade of clouded glass with a crooked fringe of beads. The whole decor was vulgar and commonplace. Heinrich Himmler had been living here, in this inelegant room, since the beginning of the year, when Hitler had threatened to dismiss him. He wore his uniform but no decorations.

Himmler greeted us with a wry smile and discussed his

* Gebhardt was executed for war crimes in 1947.

state of health; he spent a long time asking me questions about his personal life and when he would be fully recovered. Kersten then began to talk about his projects, speaking quietly and totally without expression. This discourse of his provided Himmler with an opportunity of lecturing us on honor, greatness, and loyalty, qualities which he claimed for the Germans but denied to the Slav, Mongol, and Latin races. When he mentioned the Mongols, I had difficulty in suppressing a smile, for as I had noted before, his own eyes had a rather Mongol slant.

Kersten now reacted with some heat. "But in the case of my friends Wentzel and Dr. Langbehn," he interposed, "you yourself broke your word of honor by arresting them, Herr Reichsführer, so you can hardly talk about the Germans' great sense of honor." Himmler grinned and explained that in this particular instance the special tribunal had been more powerful than he, adding that the police inquiries had clearly shown that these two gentlemen had been involved in a conspiracy.[*]

Himmler then turned to me again and talked about the predictions which I had made in respect of his own horoscope, one of which concerned an accident on December 9, 1944. "It's a strange thought, isn't it, Herr Wulff," he said, "that on December ninth I actually had an accident which might well have proved fatal. I was driving at night, and 130 feet above the Black Forest railway, I ran off the road and down the hill onto the tracks just as a train was approaching. We only just managed to get out of the way in time. The accuracy of your horoscope is phenomenal."

---

[*] This was not true, for Dr. Langbehn had been arrested before July 20, 1944, on a trivial offense, which had had nothing to do with the assassination plot.

"I am greatly reassured, Herr Reichsführer," I replied. "I did not expect the first rectification of your nativity to turn out so well. But it looks as if we have succeeded in establishing your exact moment of birth. That is a great relief. Perhaps this will convince you that you should give serious thought to the other predictions I made and consider very carefully my advice about our 'May plan.' " (The May plan was the cover name agreed upon between Himmler, Schellenberg, and myself for our projected *coup*. Kersten, who did not know the name, looked at me inquiringly with his large childlike eyes.)

"You have heard about Herr Kersten's plans," Himmler then said to me. "What do you think of them?" There was not a great deal that I could say. There were no objections to these plans on astrological grounds, and I advised Himmler accordingly.

"I can't possibly grant Herr Kersten such concessions," he replied. "He is asking for the immediate transfer abroad of a large number of Jewish prisoners. But this can't be done without Hitler's approval, because the transportation of such a large group of prisoners would not pass unnoticed and could not be kept secret from the Führer. He was horrified when he heard that my SS men were releasing Jews and gave strict orders that anybody doing so in the future was to be shot. Consequently I can authorize only some of the suggestions submitted to me in this plan."

Kersten and Storch had agreed on four major points: (1) that the imprisoned Jews should be allowed to receive food and medical supplies from abroad; (2) that all Jews should be moved to special camps which would be under the control of the International Red Cross (and which the World Jewish Congress hoped it would gradually be able to maintain from its own resources); (3) that the individual persons named on the special list which Kersten had brought with him from Sweden should be released at once; (4) that a large number of other Jewish prisoners should be released and sent abroad, initially to Sweden and Switzerland.

In this agreement a figure of 10,000 Jews was mentioned. The whole operation was being backed by the Swedish government, which had set up a headquarters in Lübeck and placed a large number of buses and trucks at the disposal of the organizers. Himmler readily agreed to the first three points on Kersten's agenda. But he refused point-blank to authorize the release and evacuation of the 10,000 Jews or of the additional Swedish, Danish, and Norwegian prisoners requested by the Swedish government. During the course of this visit I discovered that Kersten had made no headway at all during the past few days (from about March 2 on); every one of his ploys had proved ineffective. He was now afraid of falling out with Himmler altogether, for this would have jeopardized his whole project and with its his hopes of acquiring Swedish nationality.

When I asked Himmler why he was not prepared to release the Jews mentioned on the Swedish lists, he replied, "I cannot do that, Herr Wulff. The Führer already knows about the Swiss transactions involving the release of Jewish prisoners. Kaltenbrunner submitted a report about it, and his views were endorsed by Bormann. In this case my hands are completely tied." He then dropped this disagreeable topic and moved on to a new theme. "Herr Schellenberg tells me that you wish to review the political situation in the light of your mundane horoscope for 1945," he said. This horoscope was not very encouraging for Himmler. The charts for the first two quarters of the year, which I proceeded to explain to him, revealed catastrophic constellations for the Hitler regime.

Meanwhile, Kersten leaned back in the corner of the sofa, taking no interest whatsoever in my interpretations. He was aware that his personal requests had not been granted and that I had not made Himmler compliant, as he had hoped I would. His expression was neither bitter nor gentle but rather showed a studied coolness.

The conversation then turned to the Yalta Conference, which Himmler had told me to evaluate in astrological terms. I had drawn up a mundane horoscope for the Yalta Conference a month in advance. The constellations presented a positively shattering picture, which I did not attempt to soften in the telling. But, despite these hopeless prospects, Schellenberg had refused to despair and with typical Capricorn stubbornness had continued to press Himmler about his *coup d'état*. However, Himmler did not give in to Schellenberg either. He could not afford to, because his differences with Hitler had now become critical.

"Dear Herr Reichsführer," I said, "why don't you carry out our May plan? The worst consequences might still be avoided, and you yourself could improve your position despite the Führer."

"What you and Herr Schellenberg are asking of me, Herr Wulff, is a breach of loyalty," Himmler replied. "I have sworn on oath to the Führer, and although you may think it sentimental, I simply cannot break it. And have you considered the possibility of a popular revolt? How will the masses react if I arrest their Führer? True, if there should be riots in the streets, I could have them

crushed by my SS—that would not be too difficult. But I
have sworn a soldier's oath to Hitler, and I cannot break
my oath. I owe him everything. No, gentlemen, that is
impossible, I cannot do it." Himmler spoke these words
in a quiet and steady voice. As he did so, he gave me a
long, serious look and then continued:

"You say that the constellations are extremely negative
at present. Can you tell me which parts of Germany will
remain unoccupied? What does your dial say about that?"
Himmler pointed to my pocket chronometer, which I
used for a special kind of calculation to save time. Himmler had very little time left. The situation was deadly
serious. If he did not abandon his ridiculous attitude, he
would be dragged down into the abyss.

"If I remember correctly," I said, "we have already
pointed out that you should have got one of your trustworthy men to carry out our plan long ago."

"Yes, yes," Himmler interposed. "But who can be
trusted nowadays? It would be terribly difficult to stage a
*coup* now. Right now I'm not well; I feel quite weak.
From a military point of view it would be feasible, but I
cannot undertake the task. If this operation is to succeed,
I would have to replace the heads of every department;
men like Kaltenbrunner and Müller would have to go,
and they would have to be replaced by people I can trust.
Kaltenbrunner is the least reliable of them all. But if I
were to remove him and Müller, Bormann would notice
it at once and take countermeasures at Hitler's headquarters. And, anyway, Kaltenbrunner would not hesitate to
send a report to Bormann behind my back. No, it would
be far too dangerous to replace him now."

"But, Herr Reichsführer," I replied, "you could replace these men at the last moment and have Kalten-

brunner and the others arrested. I am no military expert, but I imagine that it would not be difficult for you to carry out this operation successfully."

"So now I am supposed to overthrow my Führer," Himmler exclaimed. "Herr Schellenberg even wants me to have him murdered."

In reply I referred Himmler to Hitler's horoscope: "Hitler will not die at the hands of an assassin," I said. "His constellations indicate a mysterious death. You could succeed if you arrested him."

"But how can I arrest the Führer now that he is ill?" Himmler rejoined. And then he repeated his famous dictum, which we had heard so often: "I have built up my SS on the basis of loyalty. I cannot give up this fundamental principle." And then Heinrich Himmler— a man feared by millions—said softly and almost plaintively, "I will make this confession to you, gentlemen—I simply cannot do it!"

Himmler never seriously contemplated this immense undertaking, which would have ended the dreadful and totally destructive scourge of war and brought peace and security to the world. He was too weak to make the kind of sacrifice for the country of his birth that was demanded from millions of German soldiers. He was no veteran soldier, tested in battle, who would rise up to put an end to this bloodbath. The mask he presented to the world to hide his insecurity was unctuous and mocking. He demanded sacrifices from his SS men, but where was his own sense of sacrifice, where was his willpower? Even a person with no great acumen or skill in interpreting facial expressions must surely have realized that this Heinrich Himmler preferred to allow his compatriots to suffer rather than take decisive action to relieve them.

Not even his own impending doom could make him change his mind. On that morning in Hohenlychen, Himmler barricaded himself behind the inflated fairground balloons of his own mad fantasies. I tried in vain to discover some sign of cruel grandeur in him. His face revealed no trace of the grim severity of a Spanish inquisitor or of the ferocity of the butchers of the French Revolution. Heinrich Himmler was begging me in almost pitiful tones not to press him with this frightful project, not to ask him to break with a man who had brought misery to millions of his countrymen. Fatal constellations, which were recorded in his natal chart, were now bearing down on him and could not be averted. At that moment I felt how intolerable it was to see opportunities and yet be powerless to act. I had already overcome one inner crisis in August, 1944, and now a second was building up within me. In the end I found comfort in the thought that I had done everything I could and had left nothing untried.

Himmler led a miserable existence amid the bloodstained files and card indexes at his headquarters; his life was a foretaste of hell. Scorned and despised in every corner of the world, branded as the meanest of all creatures, he was now the unhappiest of all creatures as he sat in Hohenlychen and gently begged, "Don't ask me to explain anything more, don't ask me to describe the things I have experienced and had to live through in the past few months—I can't do it!"

All this time Kersten did not say a word. I expected that he would now press Himmler for a final decision on the Jewish prisoners. But he remained silent—not for tactical reasons, not in order to present an impenetrable front, but because he was at the end of his tether and simply did not know what to do next. If Kersten had followed our conversation closely, he would have realized just how bad things were for his pitiful patient. Himmler was in need of a doctor and in even greater need of a priest. But Kersten did not budge. He simply sat there thinking about the deals which he could or—on this occasion—could not make, and as far as he was concerned, his patient Himmler, a man who already knew what it was to live in hell and was threatening to suffocate in the blood which he had spilled, was no more than a pawn in his important transactions in Sweden. Kersten was supposed to be an instrument of charity. But where were his healing hands now? In his desperate condition Himmler stood in dire need of them! But Kersten remained completely passive.

Himmler's meaningless platitudes about his loyalty sounded like a record played too often. I suddenly found the atmosphere in the room more oppressive; its confines seemed positively frightening. I looked out of the window in search of relief and saw the cheering sight of early spring sunshine glinting in the park of Hohenlychen. This was not the time to surrender myself to barren conjectures about Himmler's fate.

Himmler asked if I had received any news from Hamburg. I had already sent him a report on the destruction of the Hamburg docks, and he now learned that the reports on the bomb damage in our cities submitted to him by subordinates were far from accurate.

Next we turned to the question of armaments.

Aircraft production had virtually come to a standstill; hardly any engines were being built. How the heroic German pilots were able to continue their resistance against the superior Allied air forces was a mystery.

Himmler was aware that no new aircraft were being turned out, but the soldiers and junior officers on his staff were told that production was continuing at the same rate as before, although nobody who was at all well informed believed this.

Himmler then told me about the new air-to-air rockets and missiles which were supposed to be taking such a heavy toll of the enemy air forces. He had already spoken to me about these new weapons in the spring of 1944, when the prototypes had been built. Since then, however, it had not been possible to produce them in sufficient quantities, certainly not on the scale that would have ensured final victory. I pointed this out and asked whether it wasn't too late to cling to such hopes. I reminded Himmler of Von Rundstedt's offensive of December 7, 1944, when the First American Army had been driven back into Belgium and Luxembourg and the German air offensive had thrown the Allied troops into disarray. Although Von Rundstedt's success had been short-lived, Himmler's optimism had been understandable at that time. But today optimism was out of place. Once again I urged him to move against Hitler.

Once more Himmler excused himself on the grounds of loyalty to the Führer and went on to talk about the V weapons, which were said to be uniquely devastating. This was no mere fairy tale; the effect of the V1's and V2's was already well known—especially in Britain. But when I asked whether there were sufficient stocks of these weapons, Himmler gave an evasive reply. So it was by no means certain that they could turn the tide for Germany. There were also reports of other secret weapons that were ready for mass production, all of which tended to contribute to Himmler's vacillation.

He went on to talk about a quite different missile, one

of incredible power. Cities like New York and London, he said, could be wiped off the face of the earth with the help of this new weapon. This particular report was not entirely unfounded but meant little now that the Allies had already crossed the Rhine and the Russians had reached Küstrin, Stettin, and the Oder River and were threatening to occupy the whole of the Brandenburg region.

I had already heard about these new missiles and their enormous destructive power from Franz Göring in February, 1944. What he had told me was basically true, for work was already being done on the German atom bomb at the time.

Franz Göring also told me that the new missiles had been tested. According to him, a large town was especially built near Auschwitz concentration camp and some 20,000 Jews, mostly women and children, were sent to live in it. A single missile was then fired into the settlement. In the ensuing explosion, which developed a heat output of 6,000° C at its center, the whole town and the entire population were burned to cinders in a flash. Stories such as this also reached Himmler's ears. Was it surprising, then, that he pinned his hopes on the effect of such weapons? Was it surprising that he hesitated to depose Hitler?

At the end of our conversation Himmler again asked me for my opinion of the international situation, which I summarized in a few brief words, finishing by reminding him of our agreement and of Schellenberg's plan. Kersten and I then quickly took our leave. It looked as if Himmler were moved by our departure, for tears trickled down his cheeks, but I put this down to his shattered nerves.

The mist which had covered this beautiful Brandenburg lakeland district on our journey to Hohenlychen, transforming the landscape into vague, almost invisible forms, had completely disappeared. The warm rays of the March sun had cleared the air. We were heading for Fürstenberg. When we reached the main road, we saw an enormous mass of refugees moving westward in small groups. They were not the first groups we had encountered, and they were soon to be followed by an endless procession of human misery. When we reached Hartzwalde that afternoon, more refugees had arrived there with stories of German women who had been raped by the Russians.

Kersten avoided talking to me on the way to Hartzwalde, so I was able to work out a plan for returning to Hamburg as quickly as possible. I had thought of a reason which would justify my departure. But in the event this proved unnecessary, for upon arrival we were told that a priority telephone call had been received from Hamburg. I then learned that at midday on March 11 there had been a heavy air raid on the city, in which my own house had been completely demolished. My wife wanted me to come home as quickly as possible to arrange for the removal and storage of some of our damaged possessions. This news made it possible for me to leave Hartzwalde early the following day. That evening Kersten, who was extremely agitated because I had not complied with his wishes, tried to pick a quarrel with me. When I failed to respond, he walked out on me and retired to his own room, presumably to work on his diary. I wanted to leave Hartzwalde at once. But since there was no car available, I had to wait until the following morning. I could no longer endure Kersten's persistent demands.

CHAPTER 13

# The End Approaches

On the afternoon of April 13, after the last heavy air
raid on Hamburg, a telephone call came through from
the command post ordering me to return to Hartzwalde at
once. I was told that Himmler intended to take action.
The car placed at my disposal broke down, and the repair
delayed our departure by a day. On the evening of April
14, we left Hamburg, running into a heavy air raid at
Boizenburg. A great many trucks had been knocked out
and were scattered all over the road, together with many
dead and wounded. We only just managed to escape
harm by driving our car under some trees. Early on the
morning of April 15, we arrived at Harzwalde, where the
manageress of the estate handed me a secret report and
told me to prepare myself for an important conference
which had been convened at Schellenberg's request.

The questions which Schellenberg and Himmler
wanted me to investigate concerned Bernadotte's journey
and the proposed negotiations with Churchill, Eisenhower, or Montgomery, whose horoscopes I had already
calculated. The discussion which took place proved extremely exciting.

Toward ten o'clock Schellenberg and Dr. Rudolph

Brandt arrived. Dr. Brandt handed me a list of leading personalities in the National Socialist state who might be recommended to form a new government:

(1) Reichsleiter Martin Bormann, born June 17, 1900, at Halberstadt;
(2) Reichsminister Professor Albert Speer, born March 19, 1905, at Mannheim;
(3) Reichsminister Dr. Arthur Seyss-Inquardt, born July 22, 1892, at Stannern near Iglau;
(4) Reichsminister Count Schwerin von Krosigk, born August 22, 1887, at Rathmannsdorf (Anhalt);
(5) Generalfeldmarschall Ferdinand Schörner, born June 12, 1892, at Munich.

My astrological calculations were very difficult and I worked constantly, breaking off only to receive telephone calls from the command post and from Himmler's headquarters.

Then, on April 18, Felix Kersten telephoned from Stockholm to say that he was setting out for Hartzwalde at once with Storch. I had already heard rumors that he might bring the Jewish leader to Germany for further negotiations. April 18 was a particularly exciting day because I also learned from friends of mine in Department VI that the SS leaders, including Schellenberg, Dr. Brandt, and of course Himmler, intended to flee to southern Germany, fighting their way through if necessary. This was the "Obersalzburg plan," the details of which were revealed after the war. Himmler wanted to be near General Schörner's army, which was still intact, and I was supposed to accompany him on this trek. If I refused to go, I was to be put in chains and forcibly removed. I was deeply anxious about this proposal because the whole project was ill-conceived and ran counter to my astrological forecasts.

I was now required to investigate the problems posed by the Obersalzburg plan; this task kept me occupied for some time. Meanwhile, on April 19, Felix Kersten arrived at Hartzwalde accompanied by Herr Masur. Instead of coming to negotiate with Himmler himself, Storch had sent Norbert Masur to represent the interests of the World Jewish Congress. Masur came from a Hamburg business family who had left Germany in 1938. Kersten and Masur had flown from Stockholm to Copenhagen in a Swedish plane and had then transferred to a German plane for the second leg of their flight to Berlin-Tempelhof. In his memoirs Kersten stressed the significance of this perilous journey and the risks involved. Since Kersten was not particularly heroic and was very frightened of the Russians, this journey of his really was rather remarkable. He would scarcely have undertaken it if the Swedes had known just how far the Russians had advanced on Germany's Eastern Front; Kersten was unaware that Russian troops had occupied a number of Berlin suburbs. Masur's journey to Berlin and Hartzwalde was treated as top secret, for if Himmler were denounced, Bormann or Hitler might then intervene and have Masur arrested. Masur was to travel incognito. Himmler's personal physician, Dr. Brandt, had made out a special identity card for him, which also guaranteed his safe return to Stockholm. Masur had been authorized by Storch to enter into personal negotiations with Himmler on the agenda drawn up by the World Jewish Congress.

Felix Kersten and Norbert Masur reached Hartzwalde in the late afternoon. Earlier that morning there had been a heavy air raid on Oranienburg. Large areas of the northern suburbs of Berlin had already been destroyed, so that on their journey they passed through street after street of smoking ruins. Most of the roads were so blocked by debris that their vehicle—one of Himmler's personal cars which had been supplied by his motor transport section—had to make extensive detours and arrived very late. This was the first time that Masur—and probably Kersten as well—had ever seen such a panorama of horrors. They arrived in Hartzwalde frightened and exhausted from their unnerving experience. Masur, a small, slender man with a narrow head and intelligent eyes, had turned pale green and stood looking at us in horror. When I greeted him, he was speechless. Kersten had also lost his fresh complexion, but he recovered quickly and asked if Schellenberg had arrived. Kersten's sister Elizabeth and his secretary then took the visitors' luggage. After they had recovered, Kersten introduced me to Masur. I was not, of course, presented as Himmler's astrologer, but as a "Sanskrit researcher," in accordance with Himmler's general instructions. I was embarrassed because of my ignorance and tried to rectify matters by referring to myself as a "student of Sanskrit," for I was far from being an expert.

Meanwhile, darkness had literally descended, for as a result of the heavy raids on Oranienburg and Berlin that morning, the power and transformer stations and large sections of overhead cable had been destroyed. We sat without light or radio. Only the *A-Leitung* (direct telephone line) to Himmler's quarters was still in working order. Sleep was out of the question.

Masur opened the conversation with an account of his impressions of the journey from Tempelhof to Hartz-

walde. He was still very shaken by the terrible scenes he
had witnessed. He looked first at Kersten, then at me, and
said, "Gentlemen, we"—by this he meant the Jews—"are
all square with the Germans. We shall not try to take our
revenge. The Nazi regime was a very bad investment for
Germany." Kersten had already told me that Hillel Storch
held similar views.

But the conversation never really got going. I had been
ordered to keep quiet, and Kersten was waiting tensely
for a telephone call from Himmler's headquarters. Schellenberg had sent a message saying that he would arrive
that afternoon and wished to consult me on certain astrological matters before the discussion. But he did not
arrive.

At 2 A.M. on April 20, Schellenberg finally arrived at
Hartzwalde. The ensuing discussion was held by the dim
light of candles. Kersten immediately took Schellenberg
aside and showed him his agenda and the requests from
the Swedish government for the release of individual
prisoners. Schellenberg seemed exhausted and spoke very
little. He had not slept for days. I withdrew so as not to
disturb him and Kersten. Subsequently I learned from
Schellenberg that he had been very angry about Kersten's
demands. Kersten said very little about this conversation,
but I gathered that the Reichsführer was not prepared to
grant any large-scale concessions to the Swedes until a
date was fixed for a meeting between himself and Eisenhower.

Himmler's personal situation was very precarious, and
events were beginning to snowball. Schellenberg tried to
convince Kersten that it was in Germany's interest to persuade the Swedes to grant the German forces stationed in
Norway transit rights across Sweden so that the Eastern

Front could be reinforced. After that the conversation soon came to an end because Schellenberg was very tired and went to bed.

The next morning Schellenberg was introduced to Masur. Masur then stated his requirements, and Schellenberg agreed to them under certain conditions. But their discussion was interrupted in an unexpected way by two violent explosions. Although very few visitors to Hartzwalde were aware of it, there was an ammunition depot and a bomb disposal unit close to the estate. The fear on the faces of Kersten and Masur when the explosion occurred was something to be seen; they thought the estate was being attacked! All that was happening was that the bomb disposal men were dealing with a few fairly small unexploded bombs. Meanwhile, from the direction of the Oder bridgehead came the rumble of cannon.

Schellenberg told me that he had had no desire to join in "the madman's" birthday* celebrations and had preferred to come to Hartzwalde. Later, he said, he had to go on to Himmler's headquarters at Wüstrow and he asked me to answer some of the questions the Reichsführer had asked. In addition to the inquiries about Bormann, Seyss-Inquardt, Schwerin von Krosigk, and Schörner, Himmler wanted to know when Hitler was likely to die (this was a matter of great concern to him); whether Himmler would succeed in bringing about an armistice; whether there would be any military activity in Hartzwalde and, if so, whether this would be due to the proximity of the ammunition depot; whether the people at Hartzwalde should be evacuated; astrological profiles of SS General

---

* Hitler's birthday on April 20.

Erich von dem Bach-Zelewski, Von Alveñsleben, Walten-
horst, Professor Kurt Blome, and Balder von Schirach.

When we had finished talking, Schellenberg and I
went down to the study, where we found an extremely
agitated Kersten.

The day before, Dr. Brandt had been informed that
the negotiations with Masur would be conducted on
April 20, but since then there had been no further news,
and we still did not know for certain whether or when
Himmler would arrive. Kersten was furious when Schellenberg mentioned the possibility of a meeting with Bernadotte. "What a fool I am," he said. "I arranged the
meeting between Bernadotte and Himmler, and now all
I can do is sit here and wait!" Masur remained in the
background and kept very quiet. I found the atmosphere
wholly uncongenial and retired to my room to get on
with my work.

Just before two o'clock on the morning of April 21,
Himmler arrived. He talked first with Kersten in private.
Himmler wanted to know whether the Swedes would
allow the troops stationed in Norway to pass through
their territory. This project had been under discussion
for weeks. Kersten was supposed to have taken it up in
Stockholm and to have used his connections to influence
Günther, the Swedish Foreign Minister. But the Foreign
Minister had rejected his request. The Swedish government was prepared only to intern the German troops stationed in Norway, not to grant them transit rights. And
so Himmler had lost out again, for only Hitler could
order the troops to lay down their arms.

At this stage the military consensus was that any troops
that could be spared from Norway, Denmark, and Holland should be withdrawn as quickly as possible and sent

to the Eastern Front. But that military genius, Adolf Hitler, held a different view. His orders were to stand firm. Not a yard of ground was to be given up.

It now emerged that Kersten had no connections with Eisenhower and was unable to arrange for peace talks between Himmler and the Western Allies. Himmler still believed that the German and Allied armies ought to join forces to continue the struggle against the Bolshevists. That morning Herr Kersten declared, "This war is as much theirs as ours." But relations between Kersten and Count Bernadotte were strained, and Bernadotte was the only person in Sweden who could have established a link with the Allies. Kersten explained this to Himmler, who was relieved to hear it. It meant that he himself might still be able to negotiate with Eisenhower or Montgomery through Bernadotte. Kersten had been mistaken the day before in assuming that Bernadotte and Himmler had already met. Their meeting had been arranged for the morning of the following day at Hohenlychen.*

At the end of his talk with Kersten Himmler said, "Perhaps there will be a change of leadership soon."

That night there was another heavy air raid on Berlin. From the balcony of the house in Hartzwalde we saw the city burning in the distance. Thick black clouds interlaced with spirals of smoke rising from the exploding bombs could be seen on the horizon. However, it sounded as if a few of our antiaircraft batteries were still firing.

All this time Masur had quietly waited. Then Himmler, who had butchered more Jews than any man in his-

---

* The meeting had been set up by Kersten, at Schellenberg's instigation, when Bernadotte had visited Nevengamme concentration camp to arrange for the feeding and evacuation of the prisoners.

tory, held a secret meeting with a representative of the
World Jewish Congress to negotiate the release of Jewish
prisoners and discuss the chances of an armistice! Masur
remained cool and withdrawn.

During the course of the evening Himmler had to
promise Herr Masur that he would not carry out Hitler's
orders to have all Jewish prisoners in the concentration
camps exterminated. He kept his word and released the
majority of prisoners on Kersten's list, insofar as they
could be traced. Moreover, Himmler had no more Jews
exterminated. He is supposed to have said to Kersten at
the end of this discussion, "The best people in the nation
will perish with us; those who are left are of no interest to
us! The Allies can do what they like with those who are
left!"

At dawn Himmler and Masur walked in the fresh
morning air in the Hartzwalde grounds before taking
leave of each other. Himmler, the butcher of Jews,
walked side by side with Norbert Masur, the representative of the World Jewish Congress. Himmler said, "You
know, if we had met ten years earlier, Herr Masur, this
war would never have taken place!" Himmler then got
into his car and set out with Schellenberg for Hohenlychen.

In the course of the next few days Dr. Brandt, who had
remained at Hartzwalde, made out all the documents and
handed Kersten and Masur the necessary permits and
papers for the Jews about to be released. Dr. Brandt then
retired to his room, where he and I discussed the events
of that memorable day. Not long afterward—at about 11
A.M.—Kersten and Masur left Hartzwalde to return to
Stockholm. Kersten was angry with me because I had
been unwilling to misuse my astrological knowledge in

order to promote his personal projects. He did not come to say good-bye.

Kersten and Masur flew back to Stockholm via Copenhagen with good reason to be satisfied with their success. Heinrich Himmler had not hurt a hair of their heads. Kersten had been richly rewarded by Himmler for all the help and the physiotherapy which he had given him over the years. There were times when Schellenberg found it both embarrassing and disagreeable to obtain the large sums of money from his foreign exchange accounts and from the Reichsbank which Himmler then gave to Kersten. But Kersten knew nothing of these annoyances and would have thought nothing of them if he had. As far as he was concerned, the operation to secure the release of the Jews was a straightforward and profitable business deal in the great game of politics.

CHAPTER 14

# Heinrich Himmler's Final Orders

In the early hours of April 24, 1945, I received a telephone call from Lübeck for which I was indebted—as I learned shortly afterward—to Schellenberg's intelligent and discreet secretary. Himmler himself was at the other end of the line, and he was extremely agitated. He wanted me to come to Lübeck at once and bring the horoscopes which I had cast for various members of the government. I was somewhat at a loss to understand this order, since the SS was in full retreat and no vehicles were available. Himmler then told me that he had just received a message from Hartzwalde telling him that the refugees and staff on the estate were in danger from the advancing Russian Army. He wanted me to investigate this information astrologically and tell him my findings by telephone. He wanted to know whether it was better to evacuate Hartzwalde or to leave Kersten's staff where they were. Previously Kersten had always led Himmler to believe that the Russians were "harmless," maintaining that if he instructed his estate employees to fly the Swedish flag, nobody there would come to any harm. Meanwhile, however, the people in Hartzwalde must have had some misgivings, for they had been told by refugees from the Eastern provinces what havoc the Russians had created during their advance.

I had already discussed this question at some length with Dr. Brandt on April 21, when he had visited Hartzwalde. Brandt had agreed to my proposal that Hartzwalde should be evacuated, for I too had learned, from a personal talk with Herr Masur, about the Russians' disorderly behavior in Poland, Silesia, and East Prussia. Refugees who had arrived in Sweden from these areas had told terrible tales.

Masur had said that in the same position he would certainly leave at once and move west rather than fall into the hands of the Russians.

In the light of this information I asked Himmler to arrange for trucks to be sent to Hartzwalde at once to transport the staff and the refugees on the estate to Hamburg or Schleswig-Holstein. By then no German trucks were available, but there was a chance that the Swedes, who had sent large numbers of Red Cross trucks and buses to evacuate prisoners and refugees, might be persuaded to make the trip. At Lübeck, where the Swedish Red Cross had established their headquarters and where Himmler now was, it would be a relatively simple matter to set this operation in motion.

As a result of these initiatives, a convoy of trucks laden with refugees and the members of the Hartzwalde staff arrived at Lübeck on the evening of April 25 after a long and dangerous journey. Near Schwerin, where the convoy was attacked by low-flying aircraft, three of the Swedish personnel were killed and several vehicles damaged. Upon arrival the refugees were accommodated in quarters furnished by the Swedish Red Cross.

This relatively unimportant incident is significant in one respect, for this was the first time that Himmler, who had always been very particular about security measures, ever issued orders over the public telephone network. By then the situation was so confused that he was no longer able to use his own secret lines. Himmler himself was also confused. I gathered from our telephone conversations that the prevailing nervousness and tension had already affected him.

The meeting between Count Bernadotte and Himmler took place while Kersten was meeting with Masur.

During the meeting with Bernadotte, Schellenberg asked the count to contact Eisenhower to discuss the possiblity of an armistice on the Western Front. This request, made when the Third Reich was in its death agony, was really an impertinence toward Bernadotte. Himmler fondly imagined that after he had allowed one and a half years to pass without attempting a *coup*, the Allies would be willing to negotiate and make common cause with him against the Russians.

Himmler knew about the serious differences between Churchill and Stalin and was banking on them. But an armistice would have been possible only if Hitler had been removed, and even then, it would never have occurred to the Western powers to allow Himmler to continue in office. The most he could have hoped for was to be allowed to conduct the nation's affairs during a brief transitional period while peace was established. There were times when Himmler was aware of this. But it was clear from his eternal vacillation that he was never enough of a statesman to grasp the whole political situation. Otherwise, he would have done what had long been necessary: demanded Hitler's resignation, using force if necessary, and entered into peace negotiations. But Himmler constantly hesitated, justifying himself with inappropriate protestations of loyalty. He was entirely unaware of his tremendous responsibility toward the German people, or he would most certainly have used his

SS machine, which was still intact, to put an end to the disaster that was engulfing the nation. On April 27 the Western powers informed Himmler through Bernadotte that there could be no negotiations.

Meanwhile, Schellenberg had at last succeeded in persuading Himmler to write a personal note to Bernadotte, which he—Schellenberg—was to hand over to the count. Later the Swedish government adroitly leaked the contents of the note to the foreign press, thus ensuring that these peace initiatives were made public. This placed Schellenberg in a difficult position. Once again Himmler had tried to use somebody as a puppet without exposing himself. If the negotiations between Bernadotte and Schellenberg had had a positive outcome, Himmler would have been the great man who had brought peace to the world. If, on the other hand, they failed, Schellenberg would have to pay the penalty and might even have to reckon with the possibility of being liquidated by Himmler. Always the same old methods! But on this occasion they backfired.

Before handing the note to the Swedes, Schellenberg asked me if the constellations favored such an undertaking, whether he should now proceed with his negotiations, and whether there was a danger that Himmler might have him shot. His horoscope was available in exhaustive detail. Schellenberg was not going to die at this point, and so I was able to advise him with a clear conscience to make further contact with the Swedes. Later he could expect a fortunate period, which meant that the reports in the foreign press could not harm him, even though Himmler was likely to accuse him of going too far with his negotiations.

I was ordered to Lübeck on April 28, 1945. I was

fetched by SS soldiers and Schellenberg's personal chauffeur, Buchwald, in a crimson Mercedes. The journey to Lübeck was just like being at the front. On the main roads we saw burned-out vehicles that had been strafed in low-level attacks. Wounded men, who had escaped from these vehicles, lay on the side of the road or dragged themselves along until passing drivers took pity on them and picked them up.

Just outside the Ahrensburg railway station on the way to Oldesloe, the lines had been torn up and trains derailed. Bombed and shot-up cars were lying on all sides; lumps of iron had been scattered by the blast and lay in the fields beside the track. The spring sunshine lit up the macabre scene.

We reached Lübeck late in the afternoon. Buchwald dropped me off at the Danziger Hof Hotel, which provided temporary accommodation for the members of Department VI and Schellenberg's office staff. There I met Schellenberg's adjutant, Franz Göring. He told me in great agitation of the damage caused by the Royal Air Force in the surrounding district, and I also learned that a few of the Swedish truck convoys had been hit in low-level attacks.

It was some hours before Schellenberg arrived. "Make sure that Himmler sends me to Stockholm. Do you have all your files with you?" These were the words with which Schellenberg greeted me. He looked very tired and worn; he was trembling as he took my hand and smiled to hide his fear. We then sat down in old basket chairs with filthy cushions and broken wickerwork which creaked every time we moved. The room in which we were sitting was musty and untidy and dimly lit. The dismal atmosphere made us even more aware of the misery around us.

Schellenberg was deeply despondent, and I now discovered that it was he and not Himmler who had had me brought to Lübeck. Nobody in the department knew about his chief's problems. This was evident from the conversation which I had had with Schellenberg's secretary, Franz Göring, and various other members of his staff. Everywhere in the hotel men were hurriedly packing, stores of food were being carried about, and adjutants, SS soldiers, and orderlies were running in every direction as Schellenberg proceeded to tell me his troubles:

"The Western powers are still refusing to negotiate with Himmler, and an armistice based on the unconditional surrender of the Wehrmacht is unacceptable. How are we to carry on? The public abroad has been told through Reuters about our contacts with the Swedes and about Himmler's note. What am I to say to the Reichsführer now?" As I searched through my files for the astrological information which I needed in order to answer these questions, Schellenberg continued, "Himmler will accuse me of having placed him in an extremely difficult situation, because Hitler will now relieve him of his official posts. Everything is breaking down!"

Not a word about his own fate or that of his family, his attractive wife and his small children, crossed Schellenberg's lips. When I broached this subject, he replied briefly and nervously, "What happens to me is not so important. I still have a chance. If the Reichsführer sends me to Stockholm to negotiate the withdrawal of our troops in Norway, I shall try to arrange something with Bernadotte. Kersten will presumably have no further interest in our affairs, so there's no point in contacting him." He said this with great bitterness. Schellenberg then told me that Himmler would be discussing this project with me, for he was still looking for a way out.

I could reply only that there was little hope of changing anything and that all I could do was to speak a few words of comfort to the Reichsführer. "But I will try to discuss the cessation of hostilities in Norway and Denmark with him," I said, "and then you may be able to conduct the negotiations for the evacuation of our troops in Norway."

Schellenberg regretted that the Swedes had so far refused to grant transit rights across their territory, adding that Himmler was hoping that a favorable solution might yet be found following Hitler's death. This was, of course, the one solution which would have cost Himmler nothing and which might have enabled him to continue in office for a while as Hitler's successor, thus introducing a "stabilizing factor" into the nation's affairs, as he himself put it.

Incredible as it sounds, it seems that Himmler still thought he could persuade the Western powers to join forces with him against the Russians: that he was still so enamored of himself as to believe that the Western powers would welcome him with open arms.

He was always pointing out that Eisenhower read his SS periodical, *Die Schwarzekorps,* and claimed that the Supreme Allied Commander was well disposed toward his SS organization and troops. Statements of this kind were not optimistic, they were downright stupid, and betrayed a complete misconception of the military and political situation following the Yalta Conference. Although Schellenberg had managed to arrange a meeting between Bernadotte and the Reichsführer and—despite the completely negative outcome of their talks—was prepared to repeat the experiment, this was really no more than a comforting gesture he was extending to Himmler in the same way a doctor extends words of comfort to a dying man. Bernadotte was only interested in using Himmler to enable the Red Cross to fulfill its commitments. It had never entered Bernadotte's head to try to save him.

When Schellenberg had finished speaking, I proposed that I should retire for an hour to study the various horoscopes and establish the answers to his questions in peace and quiet. Before meeting Himmler, I also wanted to memorize the new constellations which would be emerging in the immediate future. And after all the excitement and strain of the past few days, in which I had been constantly on the move, my mental and physical powers were at such a low ebb that I badly needed an hour of solitude. About an hour later I explained my proposals to Schellenberg. There were no indications in his horoscope that his life was then in danger, but there were signs of a forthcoming journey. Thus I was able to advise him to prepare himself for a trip to Sweden and to think about who was to accompany him. After we had taken a light meal Schellenberg ordered his chauffeur to drive us to Himmler's command post.

As we walked through the hotel foyer, we were met by a warm musty wave of perspiration from the unwashed bodies of men who must have been wearing the same clothing for days on end. Exhausted refugees sat with their heads resting on the tables trying to sleep, while others squatted on their luggage and waited for transport to take them on their way. In the midst of this misery noncommissioned officers barked out orders. It was a scene of utter confusion.

We took the same road as we had taken a few days

before when Himmler himself had been at the wheel. On that occasion the passengers in the car had been extremely bad-tempered, because Himmler had just ordered General Steiner to risk an attack, a decision which had horrified Schellenberg. Since he had had no military training, his opinion carried little weight. But the military experts in the SS and Himmler's military adjutant had all agreed that further bloodshed could not do any good.

During our journey Schellenberg told me that Hitler had been in a highly critical situation for several hours. He was completely cut off from the outside world, and nobody knew whether he was still alive. "You stated in your horoscope that he would die at the end of April," Schellenberg said. "Judging by the latest reports he is both physically and mentally debilitated. But the people in his immediate circle are still blindly following his orders."

Hermann Göring was no longer a danger; his constellations were wretched. I had already established this some time before and had advised Himmler to this effect through Dr. Brandt. At that time Göring was being held prisoner on Hitler's orders. But he was too indolent a man to take strong measures in any case.

As I have already written, Reuters' report of Himmler's negotiations with Count Bernadotte had received worldwide attention. It could only be a question of time before Hitler was informed of these events. Today we know from Hanna Reitsch's account that when he was told of Himmler's treachery, Hitler raved like a lunatic.

On April 26, I had been instructed, first by Schellenberg's office and then by Brandt, to establish whether Hitler would be leaving Berlin. Contingency plans had in fact been made for Hitler to be flown from Berlin to

Berchtesgaden or, alternatively, for an SS Panzer division to break through the enemy lines and take him there overland. Like all other measures evolved at that time, these plans, which were born of utter despair, were quite impractical and had to be abandoned.

After driving through various streets on the outskirts of Lübeck, we made our way through a labyrinth of vehicles, road barriers, and huts and eventually pulled up in front of the entrance to one of these. We entered and walked down a dimly lit, narrow corridor, which ran through the middle of the hut. From the rooms on our left we heard voices dictating; from the right came the sound of heated debate intermingled with the clatter of crockery and glasses. The hut was unbearably hot, since the windows could not be opened on account of the blackout. An orderly then opened a door for us. Wooden benches ran along all four sides of the room, the wall paneling serving as a backrest; there were even benches underneath the windows. To the left of the windows stood a few beds. At the back of the room there was a large oak table, also ringed by benches. We sat down on one of the wall benches. Schellenberg ran through the points which had to be raised with Himmler. At midnight a siren sounded the all clear. Schellenberg seemed to have become more confident and had cast off the despondency that had dogged him earlier that evening.

Suddenly the door was thrown open, and Himmler, with a cigar in his mouth and accompanied by General Grothmann, his military adviser, entered the room and greeted us. I was introduced to the general. The general said a few words to Himmler and then left the room. Himmler asked us to be seated. He himself sat down at the head of the table. I sat on his left and Schellenberg on his right. Himmler's face was swollen and flushed; his eyelids were chafed. He had just eaten and smelled of liquor.

I watched him with great interest. First he asked Schellenberg to make his report. We realized that Himmler was quite distraught about the Reuters article and was convinced that Hitler would relieve him of his posts and have him arrested. He asked me what his constellations had to say on this point.

My documents and instruments lay on the table. I spread out Himmler's horoscope and the charts I needed to answer this question. And then something occurred that I found incredible and that I can only describe in plain terms, just as it happened. Himmler addressed me in a voice in which agitation was mingled with regret: "I now realize, Herr Wulff, that in urging me to arrest Hitler and enter into peace negotiations through the English you were giving me honest advice. Now it is too late. Last year, when you warned me, the time was ripe. You meant well."

Himmler then grew more and more agitated until finally, in a voice charged with fear, he said, "Now Hitler will have me arrested." This gave me my cue for broaching Schellenberg's plan for going to Sweden, which was the main point of the discussion as far as we were concerned. But Himmler, who was overwrought and deathly pale, gave me no chance to speak. He repeated over and over again, "What's going to happen? What's going to happen? It's all over!"

I thumbed through his horoscope, interrupted him, and pointed out that he still had a chance if he sent Schellenberg to Sweden to conduct fresh negotiations with Bernadotte and the Swedish Foreign Minister, and arranged to flee the country himself upon receipt of a pre-arranged message from Schellenberg.

There was a further possibility: A certain countess, half-Finnish and half-Italian, had once hinted that, if necessary, Himmler could go into hiding in Finland or Lapland. The countess was deeply indebted to Himmler, who had saved her son from execution. He liked her and had helped her on a number of occasions in her dealings with foreign authorities. This contact could now be followed up. A third proposal was similar: One of Himmler's subordinates, a certain Herr Fälschlein, was able and willing to hide Himmler on an estate in the Oldenburg district of north Germany, where he could be passed off as an agricultural worker. But Himmler, the eternal procrastinator, was unable to decide in favor of any of these proposals. When I interpreted his constellations for him he simply said, "Is that all?"

Schellenberg then began to explain his project and spoke of the new opportunities which would develop if he were able to conclude a special agreement with the Swedes on Himmler's behalf, granting rights of transit to the German troops in Norway. He might also succeed in persuading Bernadotte to arrange a meeting between Himmler and Eisenhower. This was of course a total delusion, for by that time it was far too late even to think of negotiating. I tried to make Himmler realize that after his failure to act on my earlier interpretations and suggestions, events would now have to take their course and the Third Reich would move toward its inevitable doom. But he still clung to the mad idea that having sworn an oath of loyalty to the Führer, he must honor that oath, and he then proceeded to repeat the litany that he had delivered at Hohenlychen in March. Beads of cold sweat gleamed on his face, and his body shook with suppressed sobs. In his trembling hand he held a large cigar, which he nervously pushed from one side of his mouth to the other, then removed and laid on the ashtray, only to pick it up again and frantically return it to his mouth. For a moment it looked as if Himmler had been pacified by my explanations. On my way to this meeting I had made up my mind to reproach him and to impress on him that he had only himself to blame for the present situation.

"Now you can see, Herr Reichsführer, where your procrastination has got you," I began. "Hitler will not reward you for your loyalty." Schellenberg agreed with me and pointed out that Hitler might no longer even be alive.

Although it had looked for a minute as if Himmler had regained his composure, in fact he was still quite out of control. He shouted at me, "What's going to happen? It's all over, nothing can be saved now!" Then he whispered quietly, "I must take my life, I must take my life! Or what do you think I should do?" And when I did not answer him he shouted at me in his guttural native Munich dialect, "Why don't you tell me? Tell me, tell me what I am supposed to do!" And he went on shouting the same thing over and over again.

I answered him quietly: "Flee the country. I hope you have all the necessary documents."

Schellenberg then intervened and explained to me that Dr. Brandt had taken the requisite measures for any eventuality. But he did not say what these measures were.

"Tell me what to do, please tell me what to do!" Himmler repeated, as he stood in front of me like a frightened schoolboy about to be caned, alternately chewing his fingernails and raising his cigar to his lips with trembling hands. "What am I to do, what am I to do?" he went on. And then in answer to his own question: "I must take my life; there's nothing else I can do!"

Himmler had actually made no plans. He had simply come to grief. And in this desperate situation from which there was no way out, an astrologer who had been persecuted by the Nazis and forced to live in their prisons and dark cells as a detainee was expected to advise his torturer.

At last Himmler's suppressed sobs died away, but he still chewed nervously at his nails. Then he suddenly looked at me suspiciously and asked, "What do you propose to do if Schellenberg's mission fails?"

"I shall return to Hamburg tomorrow," I replied, "and wait for the English to enter the city. We can already hear their guns on the other side of the Elbe."

Schellenberg then returned to his project, which finally received Himmler's approval.

"I'll have the requisite documents made out so that you can undertake your journey, Herr Schellenberg," he said. He then rang for an orderly and told him to instruct his secretary to draw up the necessary authorizations. He also told him that he wished to speak to General Grothmann.

It looked as if Schellenberg had been saved. But no sooner had this decision been taken than Himmler tried to reverse it and keep Schellenberg at his side. He literally clung to the man, who, for his part, was still trying, at considerable danger to himself and without a thought of personal advantage, to alleviate the fate of the German people. I now had to use all my powers of persuasion and provide relevant astrological information in order to impress on Himmler that Schellenberg's trip to Sweden was absolutely vital.

Himmler knew something about astrological techniques. He was acquainted with the fundamental principles of a horoscope and knew how to apply them. After a further hour's conversation he understood the astrological necessity for Schellenberg's mission and finally authorized it. Himmler then studied my interpretation of the horoscope, and because of the Jupiter-Saturn aspects which he found there and which he proceeded to explain with lively gestures, he gradually calmed down. He was not the slightest bit angered by the criticisms to which we had subjected him.

Considering his opportunities for action, Himmler had cut a very poor figure in the political developments of recent years. His whole attitude had been wrong. And now, even though Schellenberg had placed him in a decidedly dangerous position by his precipitate behavior during the discussion with Bernadotte on the Danish border, he still vacillated.

I realized that night that I was a complete enigma to Himmler and that he had never really understood my clear-cut astrological statements. He had twisted them to suit his own requirements. We have already seen that Himmler's offer to the Western Allies to surrender all troops under his command was published in the foreign press on April 25. The offer was made without Hitler's approval, although it would scarcely have been possible to obtain this through the confused German communications system. Himmler did not even receive an acknowledgment from the Allies. They preferred to ignore this offer from the Reichsführer and commander in chief of the SS. His offer had come decidedly late in the day. By then the Allied victory was assured.

Now, at the last moment, Himmler clung to his friends. If Himmler's health had been bad at Hohenlychen, by now it was positively pitiable. Without Kersten, he lacked both physical and spiritual solace. At that time Kersten was safely at home in Stockholm, probably sitting in front of his writing desk playing with the banknotes that he had so recently acquired. I wonder if he was thinking of his benefactor Heinrich Himmler at that moment. Admiral Doenitz was at Flensburg, discharging his duties as Hitler's deputy. He would be kept from his bed that night, for he had to sign the papers authorizing Schellenberg's ambassadorial appointment. By then Schwerin von Krosigk had been made Foreign Minister. He had been warmly recommended to Himmler by Schellenberg.

The document authorizing Schellenberg's journey to Sweden gave him full powers to enter into special negotiations with regard to the capitulation of the German troops stationed in Norway and Denmark. It was drawn up by Baron Steengracht von Moyland, Secretary of State under the new Foreign Minister, and was extremely important for Schellenberg's mission and for his negotiations with Count Bernadotte.

Schellenberg had already introduced Count Bernadotte to SS Officer Eichmann. Apart from the voluminous official index of prisoners held in concentration camps, there was only one private index in existence in the Third Reich, and that was Eichmann's. His index listed all prisoners and all political detainees from foreign countries, stating either the camp in which they were being held or the special detachment for which they were working. Eichmann knew the precise whereabouts of the majority of these prisoners and played an important part in locating prisoners during the final phase of Nazi rule.

After the question of Schellenberg's journey had been

definitely settled, Himmler suddenly had a new idea. He wanted to fly to join General Schörner's army group, which had just arrived in Czechoslovakia from the east, and await events there. He asked me what I thought of this plan. Dr. Brandt had already told me about General Schörner's plans to push forward into southern Germany from Czechoslovakia, during our conversation at Hartzwalde on April 14. He had asked me to subject this project to an astrological analysis and also to establish which part of Germany would remain unoccupied! I had then investigated both of these matters and provided Brandt with written reports. In reply to Himmler's question I now took from my file my own copy of the report on General Schörner's plan and handed it to Himmler. Its contents were not calculated to encourage him in his undertaking.

At that time two army groups were still intact and capable of resistance. General Schörner, who commanded the first of these, had recently been to Hitler's bunker at Berlin to discuss the military situation. His troops were undefeated and fully equipped. In his delusion Himmler imagined that after joining Schörner, he would be able to link up with the second of these two army groups, which was stationed in the south and led by Field Marshal Kesselring, and continue the war until the autumn of 1945. Three-quarters of the fighting forces in the south were still capable of resistance but were badly placed for the defense of either the east or the west. On April 22, it still seemed possible to use these army groups to defer the ultimate catastrophe, for that was the only thing that interested the Nazi leaders; they wanted to prolong their lease on life for as long as possible. Meanwhile, the situation had changed drastically.

Earlier Himmler had entertained the idea of flying to

Berlin to join Hitler in his bunker. Although Schellenberg thought he had managed to dissuade him from this
project, on April 25, he asked me whether I considered it
likely, from an astrological point of view, that Himmler
would still try to put this plan into effect. His first attempt to do so had proved abortive, for after reaching
Nauen, he had returned to Plön or Flensburg.

On April 15, at Hartzwalde, Schellenberg had also
asked me whether I thought he ought to attend the Führer's birthday celebrations and urged me to use my influence with Brandt in the hope that he might dissuade
Himmler from taking part; we both felt that a personal
meeting between Himmler and Hitler must be prevented
at all costs, because of the risk that Himmler might be
carried away by his sense of loyalty to the Führer. But on
the following day Brandt came to Hartzwalde with the
news that Himmler would be attending Hitler's birthday
celebrations after all. Since then the only contact between
these two had been by telephone. This continued up to
April 27.

At this point in the conversation Himmler asked me to
tell him about a number of private matters from his
horoscope. For the most part these concerned his family,
his children, and his mistress, Liesel Potthas. He then
spoke of our "friendship" and said that Schellenberg,
Kersten, and we two must stick together. After this
Himmler rose to his feet and prepared to dismiss us. As
we were leaving, he asked me whether there would be
another air raid that night. Schellenberg, who knew my
yellow list of daily planetary aspects, replied that there
would not. There were no dangerous aspects listed for
that time.

For Schellenberg the outcome of this talk was highly

satisfactory. Himmler was sending him to Sweden. He had come to Himmler with a guilty conscience, because he had already been pushing ahead with the negotiations with the Swedes to put an end to the catastrophe as quickly as possible. Now Schellenberg was traveling with Himmler's knowledge.

Himmler now left the room, and Schellenberg was told that he would receive his authorization in an hour's time. We then returned to the Danziger Hof Hotel. Our proposals for the cessation of hostilities in Norway and Denmark had been approved. Schellenberg had grown more confident and had gained fresh hope from this conversation. As for Himmler, he was waiting for the death of the Führer, news of which had not yet arrived.

I then told Schellenberg that I wanted to return to Hamburg at once. As I waited in one of the temporary office rooms allocated to Department VI for the car which was to be placed at my disposal, I heard various SS officers talking to one another; they included adjutant Fälschlein. After joining up with a group of officers from Department VI at Wesselburen, Fälschlein had asked if accommodation could be found for him at Lübeck. He and his men were clinging to Schellenberg. They all knew that the general had important connections abroad. When Fälschlein asked Himmler what he should do later on, he was told to go into hiding until such time as it was safe to come out into the open again. Fälschlein and Kirrmayer were the only people with whom Himmler was on *du* terms; they were "blood brothers." Meanwhile, my SS car had arrived and I told the driver to return to Hamburg by the Lübeck main road and not by the Autobahn. This was my last journey in an SS car, and this time I was giving the orders.

On my way back to Hamburg I thought about this final conversation with Himmler. He really was still deluding himself with the idea that General Schörner could hold out against the Allies for a considerable period. This was the very last glimmer of hope in an otherwise completely hopeless situation. Heinrich Himmler, Reichsführer of the SS, who had held forth about the heroism of the ancient Teutons to his subordinates; Himmler, the terror of the concentration camps, of the Jews, and of all those persecuted for their political opinions, wanted to crawl away like a frightened mole and hide in the mountains of southern Germany with General Schörner's army. He was just a pettifogging bureaucrat with scruples, but like his junior officers, he was true to his flag and true to his oath. His only other saving grace was economy. When it came to finances, he balanced his books down to the last pfennig.

Now, in the closing days of the Hitler Reich, he was a wanderer in a hostile world, just like his Führer, who awaited the end in the bunker of the Reich Chancellery in Berlin. When all was lost and he was safe from Hitler's vengeance, he renounced his allegiance. Then, like Hitler, Himmler escaped earthly justice by committing suicide after he had been arrested by the English in the summer of 1945. The struggle between the swastika and the zodiac had been decided. National Socialism was smashed and disappeared from the scene. Astrology in Germany, although decades behind the times, remained.